THE

PHILOSOPHY OF CREATION:

UNFOLDING THE LAWS OF

THE PROGRESSIVE DEVELOPMENT OF NATURE,

AND EMBRACING THE PHILOSOPHY OF

MAN, SPIRIT, AND THE SPIRIT WORLD.

BY THOMAS PAINE.

THROUGH THE HAND OF HORACE G. WOOD, MEDIUM.

BOSTON:
BELA MARSH, 14 BROMFIELD STREET.
1860.

THE

PHILOSOPHY OF CREATION:

UNFOLDING THE LAWS OF

THE PROGRESSIVE DEVELOPMENT OF NATURE,

AND EMBRACING THE PHILOSOPHY OF

MAN, SPIRIT, AND THE SPIRIT WORLD.

BY THOMAS PAINE.

THROUGH THE HAND OF HORACE G. WOOD, MEDIUM.

THIRD EDITION.

BOSTON:
BELA MARSH, 14 BROMFIELD STREET.
1864.

Stereotyped by
HOBART & ROBBINS,
New England Type and Stereotype Foundery,
BOSTON.

PREFACE.

A WORK of singular merit is here presented to the Public. It is but the beginning of what was designed to be a stupendous production, a comprehensive view of the whole range of the natural sciences, to be embraced *only* in the limit of some thirty volumes, of three hundred pages each! and, in the language of the author, to present a standard by which men might judge of the powers of Spirits to instruct us in the grandest truths of science and philosophy.

A concourse of circumstances not to be avoided or controlled — among which the failing health of the "medium" was the most important — prevented the continuation of the work; and, as the spirit authors were acquainted with no other medium who would be for them equally *mechanical*, their purpose was defeated from want of proper means for imparting their revelations. A few remarks may be indulged to explain the origin of the work, and the purpose of that portion which is here offered.

The writer was engaged in lecturing upon the philosophy of the "Spirit manifestations," and accompanied by the medium, Mr. H. G. Wood, of Vermont, who was accustomed to hold daily "sittings" for public investigation, when the present work was proposed to be commenced by a company of spirits, purporting to be Thomas Paine, James Marsh, former President and Professor in the University of Vermont, Ethan Allen, of revolutionary memory, and Benj. Day, and to be *written* by *one* spirit, and by Thomas Paine — the materials being contributed by all. These spirits were indefatigable in their efforts to overcome all pecuniary and other obstacles that intervened to prevent the facilitating of their purpose, and gave all directions towards the conduct of matters pertaining to their production. Several witnesses were present during the writing, who took a lively interest in the work, and rendered essential aid in assisting to carry out the directions of the spirits.

It may be here remarked, that, for some six months previous to the commencement of the writing, the spirit of Mr. Paine was almost daily present, managing all our circles with the greatest judgment, and giving multitudes of evidences which unmistakably identified him as the veritable spirit who purported to communicate.

I do not deem it necessary to enter into any details to *prove* the spiritual origin of this little treatise, though abundance of proof could be adduced; but I will content myself with simply stating that it was so produced, as the internal evidences will warrant, and that the writer purported to be Thomas Paine. That the writer was Thomas Paine, there are two convincing arguments to be offered: the one, that the chirography is a *fac simile* of Mr. P.'s; the other, that the style of composition is peculiarly his own — and that is acknowledged to be almost inimitable. The admirers of Mr. P., as an independent thinker and uncompromising writer, will be gratified to learn that Mr. P.'s residence in the spirit land has not at all either impaired his intellectual vigor, or changed his disposition to make war on all error, from whatever source it may come.

What is here presented was written with astonishing rapidity, often at the rate of a printed page per minute, and much of the time while the medium was engaged in conversation. Scarce any alteration from the original was necessary, and such changes as have been supplied are merely of a verbal character, and tautological — some errors of which latter kind still remain — which occurred from the very rapid writing, and were not regarded in the hasty copying. However, the main substance will bear as close inspection, for literary merit, as any of Mr. P.'s productions while in the flesh.

The chapters on Man, Spirit, and the Spirit Land, contain just such instructions as the present times need; and the latter two will be found to solve a multitude of problems, frequently propounded, which the infancy of Spiritual science occasions, and which the great ignorance of what has already been accomplished in the attainment of spiritual knowledge renders so mysterious.

Another chapter was commenced, which was to complete volume first, on the History of the Human Race, which promised, from what portion was written, to be of extraordinary interest. But it is deeply to be regretted that this part was not completed, for the reason before named.

The present matter is published at the urgent solicitation of many distinguished Spiritualists, before whom it has been read in MS., who pronounce it one of the best literary efforts which has yet emanated from the spiritual sphere, and as embracing within a small compass as valuable a compend of material and spiritual philosophy as has been given us from this source. Hoping that it will subserve a useful purpose in the enlightenment and conviction of many in spiritual knowledge, and the reality of Spiritual Intercourse, and thus speed the glorious revolution which is now being accomplished to bring Heaven and Earth nearer together, this work is offered with great pleasure, and with a desire that there were much more of it, by H. A. BURBANK.

CONTENTS.

THE PHILOSOPHY OF CREATION.

CHAPTER I.

INTRODUCTION.

THE world has for a long time labored under the most gross and monstrous errors, from the general indefiniteness of opinion and knowledge in reference to the creation of the Earth and the planetary system generally; and as yet, notwithstanding many different opinions have been advanced, and those too by men of science and extensive research, has the darkness, in which that point has been shrouded, been at all relieved or removed; but even now, the human mind, running back into the labyrinths of the past in search of information in relation to that matter, returns bewildered, and oftentimes infidel. Some have come to doubt their very existence, from the vagueness and mystery in which this point is involved.

It is common for mankind to regard everything as having a beginning and an end. Every *human* production *does* have, and hence the impossibility of the mind's conceiving of aught that does *not* have. Men measure everything by their own experience, and find it difficult to travel thereout for any explanations or elucidations of any mystery. It is exceedingly hard, too, for one to imagine of that point in time when *nothing* existed; and it is equally difficult, and in fact much more difficult, to conceive how *something* could be created out of *nothing;* and yet it is claimed by a large class of men, that *God,* in the plenitude of his power, called forth the infinitude of worlds, that at this day are sweeping through space, from nothing. *Alike* created space, matter, worlds and laws, *where* nothing, and *when* nothing existed. Men who entertain those notions, as many *do,* and *honestly* too, exhibit remarkably small and contracted reasoning powers.

It may not be amiss, in this place, to explode the scriptural account of creation, and hence destroy the basis of the fore-mentioned opinion. It is claimed that in six days God created the heavens and the earth, and upon the seventh rested; and let me say, without any irreverence for Deity, that if he *did* create the Earth in six days, he *needed* to rest upon the seventh. But the question *is, did* he create the Earth in six days? I answer, *no. Data,* independent of any I shall bring forth to substantiate this proposition, gathered by men of science *in* the flesh — *data,* too, that no man sees fit to deny — plainly show that matter originally existed in a liquid state, and that it remained in this state for millions of years. And, *too,* that the planet Earth for millions of years existed, before it was prepared for the reception of animal or vegetable life. Not because it did not contain within itself the elements necessary to produce and support it, *but* because those elements had not been reduced to the proper condition necessary to generate and support life. Each different state or condition of matter has possessed its different powers to generate and sustain life, and hence, in various ages and periods of Earth's existence, different species of animal and vegetable life have existed. Fossil remains of animals and vegetables, at this day found in various portions of your Globe, in the different formations, show plainly that no less than seven times has the whole course and kind of life, both animal and vegetable, been changed; and, *too*, that these changes have been millions of years in being effected. Now the fact is here, either Science or the Bible is false. Which will you accredit? Science is based upon well-known *data*. The Bible is *entirely*, wholly, in this instance, based upon imagination. It is the mere creation of a wild and sickly fancy.

One strong evidence that may be brought against the scriptural account of creation is the fact, that all through that Book not one word is said of any other world than this. But from it you are left *to*, and legitimately *may* draw the inference, that the Earth is the only planet existing, and that the various other worlds, there called stars, &c., are merely balls of fire hung in the heavens as lamps to light and warm the Earth, incapable of generating or supporting life. In a word, that this planet is the favored of God, and the grand theatre of his wisdom and skill. I say that this inference may be drawn legitimately, because it is there expressly stated that God created the Earth, then he created Day and Night, the Sun to rule the day, and the Moon and Stars to rule the night.

Astronomers tell you that the sun, moon and stars are worlds, composed of elements like those of earth,— some of *equal*, others of *greater* magnitude than earth; and moreover, that, while the earth is lighted, &c., by those planets, they likewise are lighted by earth. The earth is but *one* of an indefinite number of worlds, forming a vast planetary system.

From the innate properties of matter any sensible man would infer that these various worlds must be the theatres of life, of animal and vegetable life, adapted to their various situations, conditions, &c.; and indeed it would be a disparagement of the wisdom of God, to suppose that all these worlds were created by him without object or aim; for I can confidently assure you that *many*, very many of them are so remotely located from the earth, that it is neither favored nor benefited by their light. Were they created without an aim, without an object? I answer, no. God never created aught unless to subserve an end.

But I do not wish you to understand, by *this*, that everything is immediately created or brought into existence by God; but that all of animal as well as vegetable life comes into existence by the force of natural laws, of certain principles *in*, and properties *of* matter, that necessarily generate the peculiar species of life that exist. That different conditions of matter, the different states of situation, &c., have a strong and peculiar influence upon the species of animal and vegetable life extant, is evident to your senses, from the fact, that even upon your own earth, in different parts, there are *different*, widely different species of life, peculiar to the climate, soil, &c., and which removed from their peculiar localities would die.

I might here proceed to state various facts to show that matter has within itself elements, which, peculiarly united or brought together, necessarily produce life — animal life. For instance, in stagnant pools there is generated a peculiar animal of a spiral form, called the *Rotifier Redivivus*, which in *its* element exhibits a remarkably lively existence. Take this animal from its element, lay it upon a shelf and allow it to dry, and to all appearances die, and in fact to be *actually* dead. Let it lie there for years, and then replace it in its element, and its life will return; it will not indeed be animated by the same spirit, the same life, as it originally was; but, being brought again in contact with its natural elements, it receives another spirit or life, and hence moves, lives.

Another simple illustration of the properties of matter to generate life is here. Take wheat flour, and with the same unite resin: boil them together in water, and let the preparation stand for a few days, subject to the action of heat and cold, and there will appear upon the surface a peculiar kind of animal, that will live only so long as it is subjected to the action of heat and cold. I might cite hundreds of instances, but I will wait until I am further advanced in the work before me, when I intend to give a general explanation of life of all kinds, and under all conditions. But I have already cited enough to establish the fact, that *all* matter is possessed of a spiritual principle, or of life-creating principles which, when under different circumstances and conditions united, give birth to various kinds of life.

Animals and vegetables alike are endowed with spirit; — without spirit nothing can live. Remove from matter its spiritual principle, and it will at once decay, and be taken up by other living matter and be reänimated; —hence the conclusion, that wherever there is matter there will be life, or the necessary elements to produce and sustain life; hence, too, the inference in your minds, that the various planets are the theatres of animal and vegetable life, as I have before said; and hence, likewise, the absurdity of the Biblical account of creation. There is no need of entering into a more elaborate argument upon this point, as the common sense of mankind is already beginning to lead them to search after more substantial and satisfactory food.

CHAPTER II.

DEITY.

As I approach this important branch of my subject, I would desire the readers to lay aside their various prejudices, and for a while to indulge with me in a little reasoning upon the matter.

Mankind have ever had peculiar and strange ideas of God. Each man has had his own God — a God of his own creation and imagination. Each one has created in his mind a God peculiar to himself, and in accordance with his mental condition. There *are*, and always *have* been, as many different Gods, as there are or have been different human beings. Could I expose to your mental vision the different Gods as they have existed in *idea*, I should expose to your gaze a picture such as your eyes never before beheld; but it is not my task or duty so to do. I will simply proceed to an inquiry in relation to him.

In the first place, then, let us inquire who and what is God? The general idea has been, and in fact still *is*, that God is a *person;* but I will here assert that this is fallacious, and the absurdity of this idea is evident, from the fact that it is said that God is omnipresent, by the same individuals who assert that he is a person; for if he is a person, existing in form, he would not by any possibility be omnipresent. God is not a person, but a *principle*, the all-animating principle of all things.

Deity is generally regarded as the *author* of *all* matter, but instead of that, he is a *principle* of matter. It is said in Holy Writ, as it is called, that no man has ever seen God, nor ever will. This is well said, and for the support of that book was *necessarily* said. God is eternal, ever *has* and ever *will* exist; but he is no more eternal than matter, for both are eternal, as they are coëxistent. There is nor was no grand architect of the universe or universes, aside from him; for he is the great first cause, or grand centre of all intelligence, permeating all matter, and the living, intelligent principle therein. The grandest and most perfect existence. *The* perfect and *only* perfect existence. The grand centre of all perfection, and of all spiritual attributes.

To give mankind a correct idea of God would be beyond the power of language: his attributes exist, but words cannot sufficiently strongly set them forth. His works are all around you, and *in* his works you can see *him* and his power. If by works you are to judge the author, what *cannot* be said of God? Mankind are measured and reverenced in proportion to the intellectual power and skill exhibited in their various productions; and yet *man* is but a small *iota* of God. If you pay homage to human intellect, which is but an iota of the *grand intelligence*, what homage is due, or rather what homage is not due to the *grand* intelligence?

I wish to be understood, however, that God is naught but a *principle*, and that too of *necessity*. He *can* exist, does exist, but cannot, by any possibility, *cease* to exist. He is an innate quality *of*, and principle *in* matter, that will exist long after matter has been reduced to a spiritual state — for the tendency of *all* matter is to perfection or spiritualization — approximation to Deity.

As I have before said, I can give you no adequate description of Deity, as there is no language in which and with which I can paint to you his attributes. But that there *is* a God, a Deatific principle, there needs no words nor assertions of mine to prove. No one, who for a moment surveys the wide domains of nature, beholds the myriads of worlds sweeping in space above, about and around him, with the utmost regularity and precision; who beholds, both in the animal, vegetable and planetary systems, the perfect adaptation of all things, each to the other; who contemplates the perfect laws by which all things are governed and controlled;

can for a moment doubt, but there is existing somewhere in the realms of space, an intelligence, that has assisted and guided in the production, construction and control of the infinitude of created things. Let him, who has for a moment doubted the existence of God, contemplate himself, ask himself whence he came? how he was created? whence his superior intelligence? and he will return from his reflections firm and unwavering in his faith in the existence of a central intelligence.

Whence came intelligence, if it has not ever existed? Can matter create intelligence? Impossible. It contains within itself a grand *principle* of intelligence, that is coëxistent with it, but it cannot, and does not create it. There are certain properties in matter, which, when peculiarly united, generate life, which life in its various stages exhibits intelligence; — can it be said that this life and intelligence were created by matter? Most certainly not. This life and intelligence were produced by a union of properties, in matter, that ever existed. Matter ever *has* and ever will contain within itself these properties — Life and Intelligence in embryo. Now whence comes intelligence, unless it wells up from a grand fountain seated in the realms of matter, pervading every part of the universe and universes in existence? When one can answer that question differently, then may he well doubt the existence of God; until then he must admit his existence.

Now the question comes up for our contemplation, what influence did Deity have in the formation of worlds, &c.? But of this portion of my subject I will treat more extensively by-and-by, when I approach another branch of the treatise. I will now simply proceed to speak of the origin of a belief in God, and also of the various ideas which are rife in reference to God, and of the cause of the extreme difference of opinion concerning him.

There is in man a principle of intelligence, that naturally leads him to regard all existing things as having an author; — hence, among all people, and in all times, and under all conditions of intellect, this belief has existed, and in various degrees of perfection. The attributes of God have varied as the condition of human life has varied. The aborigines of this country had their forests peopled with the Great Spirit, who presided over their destinies, guarded their wigwams, their hunting-grounds and their souls; who held them in charge in their conflicts with enemies. When the thunders bellowed and the lightnings flashed, they supposed the Great Spirit angry, and hence, in those times, they attempted to conciliate his favor by various manners that they believed to be pleasing to him. When any misfortune came upon them, they regarded it as an evidence of the displeasure of the Great Spirit. When they were successful in the chase or in war, they regarded it as an evidence of his pleasure. The Indian's God was a God possessed of attributes compatible with the Indian's mind. He was regarded to be a kind father, so long as his children were obedient and good, but as fierce and inhuman, when they were disobedient and bad. He was a revengeful God. He was given this attribute by them simply because they themselves were *naturally* revengeful, and hence they supposed of necessity that God must be so. The Indians, like every other people, created for themselves a God possessed of the highest attributes of which their minds could conceive, and clothed him with virtues, such as they themselves practised, or supposed they ought to practise. Brutality in war, revenge, &c., being regarded as virtues by the Indian, he naturally created in idea a God possessed of these attributes. So every tribe and nation of the Earth has its God, and that God may *invariably* be measured by the intellectual growth and culture of the people.

The truth is, every man's mind naturally turns to some superior being to whom he desires to pay homage, some being to whom he can allege the cause of everything; some creative and controlling power higher than himself: and that being will ever be just in accordance with the intellectual state of the person. He will be a being possessed of powers and qualities refined or gross, just as the intellect of the man is refined or gross. The savage has his God, and oftentimes desires something tangible, something that he can *see*, *feel*, &c.; hence many, even at the present day, being possessed of a low intellectual state, fall down and worship Gods of wood and stône; others worship the sun and moon; others, various animals, as the elephant, &c.; — and indeed a people may ever be judged, mentally and morally, by their ideas of God and religion.

The God of the Christians, or of Theologians of the present day, should be a being possessed of great powers and noble attributes; but I am sorry to say that at this day, civilized people, who have had the advantages of the arts and sciences, entertain most ridiculous and absurd notions of him; clothe him with attributes entirely antagonistical and inhuman. They make him a God of Love and unacquainted with Evil, and yet a God revengeful and barbarous; a being possessed of all wisdom, and yet one of the most silly and imprudent beings in existence; and, at the same time, this God corresponds with the training, the mental and moral condition of those who entertain these notions.

But I need not proceed further to prove to you that God is a creature of *idea*, and a being of whom no one has a very exalted or satisfactory knowledge; for the idea, that there is a *being*, who created and presides over the grand economy of Nature, is fast disappearing from among you; and soon will the world be willing to listen to the voice of Reason, and believe that God is not a *being*, but a principle, as I have before said. Then will the heathenish ideas, that at this time are entertained, vanish, and the clear sun-light of Reason stream full upon the mind, enlightening and liberalizing it with the genial influence of Truth. The great errors of the day—*popular* errors—will be dispersed, and mankind approximate to that grand Harmonial state that is so compatible with nature, and so necessary for the heavenizing of the universe. Then will mind, freed from the fetters by which it has been for ages bound, soar away into the domains of nature, to gather up the innumerable gems that are there hidden in the depth of matter, brilliant and elevating in their tendency, to deck and adorn its existence. Then will fade away and entirely disappear that class of men, at this day called spiritual teachers, whose labors are, and ever have been, directed toward the promulgation of absurd errors and false religion, and mankind be taught by the principle within called Reason, and the principle without called Nature.

CHAPTER III.

SPACE AND MATTER.

SPACE is but a condition of matter; and hence, matter being eternal, it must be an eternal condition. Matter could not exist without space, hence it *is* a *necesssary condition* of matter; but matter is not a *necessary* condition of space, for without matter space could exist. Space is infinite to the human conception; it has no bounds, no end, but rolls away even beyond the conception of spiritual beings. It is the theatre of worlds, whose number is infinite, and entirely beyond human power to compute or comprehend. The theatre of worlds, or life, is not bounded by human vision, either aided or unaided by the powers of art. No optical instruments will ever enable the human eye to range its immensity, to see or comprehend one octillionth part of the number of worlds that are there making their revolutions with precision and regularity.

A great mistake is usually, and ever has been here; people have ever supposed, and in fact still do suppose, that the Earth is the only inhabited planet, and was the first world made capable of being inhabited; but this is not true, for there are worlds that were created long before the Earth, and which became the seat of human life, long before the Earth had ever borne the most gross kind of mineral or vegetable life; and where the arts and sciences had attained quite an eminence, before the Earth even had a separate existence. I shall be able to demonstrate this fact to you before I close.

This idea in reference to the Earth was originated, and existed from a blind faith in the Scriptures. If that Book is true, there can be no other inhabited planet; as man is there taught that Earth is God's favorite land, and the only spot where he has made an exhibition of his power, either in the formation of worlds, or intelligent beings; — in a word, that all the other worlds in existence were created merely to serve the Earth by their light, heat, &c. But the fallacy of this idea has already been exploded by astronomers, — yet mankind, notwithstanding the many contradictions of Biblical accounts by science, seem disposed to hug their Idol to their hearts, to be yielded up only when necessity compels. Reason and Truth are alike rejected, and the most absurd and ridiculous errors are recorded with their creeds. But I am travelling from my subject.

I have before stated, and will now re-state, that *matter is eternal,* — ever has, and ever will exist; and hence it follows, as a necessary consequence, that all the qualities, properties and developments of matter, are equally eternal, existing *in,* and a necessary attendant *of* matter — though in an embryo or latent state — to progress and attain perfect development, only as matter was impelled to progression by its interior forces; for as matter *progresses,* the laws that govern it obtain force, *added* force and conspicuity.

Pervading all matter, even to its minutest tissue, was the great intelligence, whose power is and was unlimited to the human conception, aiding and assisting in *urging on* the grand work of progression, development and formation. The power, exerted by this intelligence in this grand work, language cannot describe, nor human power in the remotest degree comprehend; but yet to him all things were obedient, and his mandates were law. Acting by regular laws, progression followed, and the grand ultimates in due time appeared, in perfect or imperfect states of existence, as they were developed in earlier or later periods of progressive existence. There were in matter embryo systems and worlds in infinitude, together with the power of forming, governing and locating them.

Perhaps one of the most important powers of matter was the power to throw off or rid itself of all refuse matter, or that matter which was not useful in the grand economy of production; which power ever existed in matter, but was not developed until a late period of its existence, or that period of its existence when it had become prepared to be formed into systems and worlds, when it came forth from the latency in which it had slumbered, and exhibited its full vigor and usefulness. This power of matter exists now, and will account for the appearance of those erratic bodies that are now and then seen wandering in the immensity of space, apparently without location or laws, in the grand system of the universe, called comets. They are fragments of worlds, rejected as drones, and sent off to provide for, and locate themselves; — possessing within themselves the elements and powers to produce worlds, and take a stand as such in the category of the universe, — and ultimately they do. The Earth itself was once a wanderer like them, possessed of undeveloped elements, tossed about upon the bosom of immensity, to find a home and location for itself. These bodies frequently approach so near *to*, as to be taken up *by* the Sun, and thus go as fuel for the supply of light and heat to the various worlds dependent upon it therefor.

Matter and power are coëxistent; and as motion is a direct effect and consequence of power, and must have followed simultaneously in its path, it follows that Matter, Power, and Motion, are coëxistent.

The primitive or original condition of all matter was liquidity. This is demonstrated from the oblate spheroidal form of your Earth, which could only have been the result of the motion of the Earth in a liquid condition, when, from the greater rapidity of motion in its centre than at the poles of its axis, this form would naturally and necessarily follow.

Could the human eye behold matter in its primitive condition, it would behold swelling far away into the immensity of space, apparently without bounds, and without laws or order, a vast unparticled mass of liquid fire; a vast receptacle and theatre of contending elements and latent worlds, — unawakened laws and undeveloped forces, — apparently without particles, without forms, because it was one grand unparticled mass of combined Suns, Systems and Laws, in an embryo or latent state; — but could your vision *penetrate* this mass, you would behold, permeating *all* its parts, a positive power, whose grand object and duty was to arouse latent energies of elements to progressive action.

The original condition of matter being liquidity, heat and light must have been the primitive developments; and as an important agent in formation, and as a direct effect of heat, Magnetism followed in the train of developments.

Matter having originally formed one unparticled mass, of course it was not subjected to the action of *external*, but only internal forces; hence it floated on the bosom of immensity unmolested, save only by the forces that were internally acting to prepare it for the grand development of Systems and Worlds. It must be borne in mind, that though matter was originally one *unparticled* mass, it nevertheless contained within itself embryo particles to infinity, which waited simply for the action of necessary forces for their development. This grand mass contained no regular form, as *it*, by the force of its interior elements, was continually undulating in space, and hence changing its form as those undulations were increased in rapidity.

The first, or original form, assumed by matter in the course of formation, was the angular or *crystalline*, which was the result of angular or crystalline motion, together with forces of which I shall soon speak more extensively. Magnetism followed in the train of developments, as a necessary development of heat, and hence Electricity obtained an existence, — hence was established in matter, in development, a positive and negative power, Magnetism being positive, and Electricity negative. Magnetism is a principle, because the result of the development of a principle, that is, heat;

but electricity is but a condition or negative state, induced by an absence of heat, or by cold.

These agents, permeating matter, infused into it an electrical power or state, that was exceedingly important in the grand work of particulation and formation, immediately destroying the extreme intimacy, *fraternal* intimacy, before observed, throughout the infinitude of matter, and making enemies and friends in a twinkling, which occasioned each of a kind to seek the other, and to array themselves as 't were for a grand conflict.

From the development and action of these agents, the work of development went rapidly on, until that point was attained, when, by the action of internal forces, a large portion of this immense mass went whirling away into the immensity of space; and then commenced a mighty change in the condition of matter. A mighty disturbance was there; — the great chain of union was broken; slumbering powers were awakened from their dormancy, and came into vigorous and active employment; new laws gained force, the great mass commenced to reel, and one system after another broke away, in endless succession, from its parent mass, and, taking with itself a grand centre or sun, rolled far away into the bosom of immensity, to assume and occupy an independent and separate existence. System after system, world after world, was thus evolved and sent off, until the illimitable expanse of space was apparently filled. Rolling away in its infinitude, erratic and irregular, they at last, by the power of gravitation, were located, and then commenced the grand work of internal development.

The number of systems and worlds evolved, the

human mind could not comprehend, — their number is infinitude. But systems being formed, laws established, and worlds located, in each world evolved, particulation and general development commenced. The internal together with the external forces, acting upon each, occasioned revolutions *upon* and *around* a common centre, that was essential to a full development of the powers of matter.

These revolutions were occasioned by the magnetic powers exerted, each upon and by the other, that gave rise to what are commonly called centrifugal and centripetal forces, or the tendency of matter to fly *from* and *towards* a common centre. The magnetic forces, exerted by the surrounding bodies upon each other, gave rise to the centrifugal, and the magnetic power of the particles, one over the other, or their *affinity* for each other, occasioned by their electrical conditions, together with the influence of motion, gave rise to the centripetal; and thus matter has the power within itself to keep up or maintain an equilibrium, even among contending forces.

Being established in space from the influences exerted upon each other, together with the power of internal forces, each world began first to move upon its axis in a circular form, and then about its common centre the Sun; and each system performed, and performs its revolutions around other systems; hence there is a continuation of circular motion observed by worlds and systems to infinity, occasioning Day and Night, seasons, &c., in each proportioned to the length of time occupied in its revolution upon its *own* centre, and around the grand systemal centre.

This revolution upon axes occasioned, as a matter of course and necessity, the spheroidal or globular form exhibited in each World, and also the globular particulation of *matter*. All matter, from the first second of systemal existence, was, from its magnetic condition, endowed with a disposition to fly *from* and cling *to* its common centre, which, as a necessary consequence, produced globular particulation; hence, while each world is itself a *grand* globe, its *minutest* particles are *equally* globes.

The original condition of matter could not have given rise to this globular form of particles, as there was then no external force operating upon it; hence there was no tendency *to* nor *from* a centre, but a perfect equilibrium in all parts. The grand mass rolled upon no axis, as there was then no force to give it circular motion, — circular motion was then undeveloped; — but when, by the force of internal powers, one part of the mass flew away, there was set up and exerted an external influence, that would put into requisition the powers of motion; and hence, for a succession of ages, one system after another was being formed during each successive second, and thrown away upon the sea of space to travel to its proper location, until throughout the whole endless expanse there was set up an equilibrium.

The time occupied, in the establishment of this equilibrium, cannot be conceived by the human mind. For, could you travel with the rapidity of light, you would never be able to approach the remotest worlds seated in space. Hence an endless period was necessary for the performance of the journeys performed by these innumerable systems to their allotted destination.

The time occupied in the making up and throwing off of these systems from the grand mass is equally incomprehensible; and it were a needless task for me in the remotest degree to attempt to impress it upon you. The human mind is incapable of conceiving the immensity of space, and of the immensity of that grand central mass, from which *all* systems and worlds sprung. The mind cannot conceive infinity, — space is infinite, without bounds or limits.

The original masses thrown off were without regularity of form, and not until a perfect equilibrium was established, did any assume, or nearly approximate to the spheroidal form; but systems taking location, the established forces acted upon the members of the *system*, and revolutions commenced. The extremely rarified condition of matter, at that period, prevented *rapid* motion, as the *full* force of the magnetic power could not be experienced in that condition; but as the bodies revolved and rarification decreased, the motion increased in rapidity, until perfect regularity of motion was established.

Matter possesses within itself the power to throw off all refuse matter, or that which is not needed in the grand economy of production; hence new systems and worlds are, and were continually being evolved, but at such remote distances from *established* systems, as hardly to exert an influence thereupon.

Matter has within itself, also, all the elements necessary for the generation and support of both animal and vegetable life — which power is progressive; and hence, in different periods of its condition, different kinds of life would be produced. In its extremely gross state, equally gross vegetables and animals would be produced; but as it *refined*, life of *all* kinds would keep pace with its progression.

From the preceding propositions it follows that *all* systems and all worlds have inherent within themselves the power to generate and support vegetable and animal life; hence each has the power to produce all the elements, as air, water, &c., so necessary in the grand economy of life.

These afore-mentioned elements were produced, or generated, before *life* could have commenced; hence, as they could not be generated until the mass had thrown off its heat, and assumed comparative coolness in its particles, it follows that life was not, nor *could* be generated, until the earth had become *encrusted* upon its surface, or cool.

In the productions of *all* existing things, air, water, life, &c., magnetism and electricity were the efficacious and indispensable agents. These agents, traversing the realms of matter, by virtue of inherent laws, impregnated each embryo particle with an electrical condition, that made it subject to the laws of attraction and repulsion, which by no possibility could they suspend or disobey. Magnetism being positive, and electricity negative, attraction and repulsion followed as a natural result; — hence particulation began, and the various gases, fluids, &c., obtained existence.

In the primitive condition of matter, heat possessed no disposition to travel, for there being no *external*, but only internal forces acting, the grand attraction was to the mass, — there was no power to impel its rays, and no necessity for their impulsion. But when systems were established, and the laws thereof shook off their latency, heat was impregnated with a disposition to fly off, in straight lines, into the grand receptacle of immensity, and hence *cooling* commenced in matter.

From this point matter commenced rapid progress. For millions of years the red rays went streaming away into the grand vortex of immensity, until the earth began to lose its heated state *externally*, and form itself into proper conditions. The atmosphere was developed, vegetable life was generated, and minerals went to their proper beds. But yet the grand centre was not cooled, nor by any possibility could it be; for the extreme condensation of particles, attendant upon the establishment of gravitation or weight, naturally produces and maintains heat: hence, at this day, and to all eternity, the centre of your Globe will be one mass of liquid fire. It is an essential condition in the economy of production, and seems to have been an arrangement of the positive power.

The fact of the liquidity of the centre of the earth — if not sufficiently evident from the natural results of condensation — will appear from the frequent eruptions of volcanoes, which are occasioned and fed by a disturbance among the internal fiery elements. These fires *must* have vent; and in earlier periods of the world, when the crust of the earth was less hard, more frequent eruptions happened, and at more near distances. Volcanoes are essential outlets of these fires, for were they not allowed to escape in that manner, earthquakes and dire calamities would come quick and fast upon you.

Though, in the production of earthquakes, electricity is usually a powerful agent — magnetism being a development of heat, and electricity being a negative condition, or the result of the absence of heat — it follows, of course, that electricity was an efficacious agent in the cooling of the earth.

In the course of particulation, electricity occasioned the development of elements. Endowing all matter with an electrical condition, positive or negative, the various developments of matter followed. Each substance of like properties, or of a kind, sought its kindred, in the general confusion of elements, and hence combination and formation was continually going on; — hence, many of the phenomena, exhibited in rocks, of *veins* of quartz, gold, silver, iron, and various other substances, foreign to the general body of the rock, may be accounted for. The existence of these will serve as a conclusive evidence to your minds that the great mass of matter must, primitively, have been in a state of fusion, as in no other possible way could these depositions in veins have been made. Rocks are frequently found by you, in which veins of iron, gold, &c., exist, that run for many miles in the rock, and frequently its entire length.

Minerals are usually found in substances to which they seem peculiar, as gold and silver are found in quartz, &c., which plainly shows that minerals were not *primitive*, but ultimate developments of matter — of *peculiar* matter, which, by the property of matter to throw off all refuse matter, or that not used in the economy of production, occasioned these particular depositions of minerals; and yet they were the first developments of motion, because the first substances that assumed form — they assuming the *crystalline*, or primitive form. Minerals I shall treat extensively of in another part of this work — more particularly in future volumes.

The extension of rocks of particular species, as marble, &c., in particular directions, — oftentimes in continuous chains for hundreds of miles, — demonstrates the proposition, embodying the fact, that particles sought their kindred; and the frequent recurrence of veins and traps, in these rocks, of different species, demonstrates the chaos and confusion in which the elements originally were.

Could the human eye behold the earth after its establishment in the solar system, it would behold a vast body of liquid fire, whirling through space, in wild and chaotic confusion. Could it *penetrate* the mass, it would behold a disturbance of elements, such as the mind cannot conceive, or language express. But there was a running to and fro of elements, and the action of forces, which, in future periods, were to bring forth from this awful confusion perfect symmetry and form, progression and development. There were powers in that mighty chaos that would not yield; positive influences, whose mandates must be obeyed, and which were destined to tame the confusion, and bring forth perfect order.

The tendency of matter is progression. Its ultimate is Spirit; — hence, in the train of mineral developments, and developed by the innate properties of matter, came the vegetable developments. In vegetables is exhibited the *circular* motion, which was developed by the *crystalline.*

The tendency of matter being progression, and the original condition being gross, it follows, as a necessary consequence, that the original condition of the vegetable kingdom must have been exceedingly imperfect and coarse; and this truth will appear more evident, from the fact that the vegetable kingdom was partially developed before the elements had been brought into harmony and order, as is manifest to you from the fact that remains of vegetables, now extinct, are found, embedded even in the body of solid rocks, that could only have been formed by an igneous agent, as also far down in the bosom of the earth, evidently and really placed there by *water;* and the different species of vegetables, found in the formations, plainly show that there has been an entire change in the vegetable kingdom for many times, — which is an evidence of the progressive power of matter.

The first species of vegetables developed were of a coarse, large order, entirely, widely different from the state of vegetables at later periods, and in different formations, and from their condition now. The materials that entered into the composition of these vegetables — which were principally of a marine order, with few land plants — were also different. Development, then, had not attained to perfection, but was merely on the threshold of progression, of a progression to which it was to be subjected through and during countless centuries. As the mineral developed the vegetable, so the vegetable developed the animal kingdom.

That there was a wide difference in the elements and condition of the vegetable kingdom, will appear evident to your minds, from the fact that, during the earlier periods of matter, the materials of the earth were less dense than subsequently, and, consequently, that the elements therein had a less perfect power; as, also, from the fact that the atmosphere, light, heat, and water, have a strong influence upon plants, and give rise to perfect, or less perfect developments therein, as they act upon them in a perfect or less perfect manner.

The atmosphere, in the earlier periods of the earth's existence, had not been reduced to its present chief elements, but was also filled with other elements that now are unknown therein. It was then less rare — more dense than now. Water, also, was then in a more dense state, being composed of less hydrogen and more nitrogen, as also fluorine, which is the result of a union of hydrogen and nitrogen, and also carbon. This proposition can hardly be denied by men of science and research. It certainly will not be denied by those who acknowledge the progressive tendency of matter. There cannot be found a substance which does not possess these elements in a greater or less proportion.

The relative position of the Earth, in reference to the Sun, in its primitive condition, being widely different from now, made a great change in the degree of light, as also of heat received from that body; — from all which facts it will appear that the vegetable world has undergone wide changes.

The animal being developed by the vegetable, and dependent thereupon for existence and support, must have partaken of the nature of the vegetable, and hence, in its primitive stages, have been equally gross and imperfect, which is demonstrated by fossil remains found in various portions of the Globe.

The first kinds of animal life developed, worthy of notice, were of the *polyparia*, fish, and *saurian* species, which, passing through regular stages of gradation and perfection, ultimately gave rise to, or developed species of a higher or more perfect order, as the vegetable world was perfected or progressed.

Having now traced the Earth, in a cursory manner, up to the development of the three kingdoms, it behoves us to go back and examine, in a more minute or particular manner, its condition and appearance, during its primitive and subsequent periods, in order that you may be able to comprehend propositions, in relation to the three kingdoms of Nature, that it will be my province, in a more progressed part of the book, to advance and support.

CHAPTER IV.

THE PRIMITIVE CONDITION OF THE EARTH.

We have traced the progress of Creation *generally*, up to the establishment of the Systems, and the Earth *cursorily*, up to the development of the three kingdoms; we will now return, and more minutely trace the progress of development, together with the causes producing the various conditions, primitively and latterly holden by matter. We have seen that, though matter originally existed in a chaotic, or confused state, it nevertheless had within itself the *elements* of all mineral, vegetable, and animal developments, and their necessary attendants, appurtenances, &c.

The Earth was originally comprehended *in*, and formed a part *of* the Sun, and hence was, for a long period of time, subjected to the action of the external forces acting upon matter, after the general confusion of formation had begun in a degree to subside. It was thrown off from that body by the force of external and internal agencies operating upon that body. It may be proper and essential that we should now stop to inquire what these internal agencies or forces were, or what it is and was that gave to matter the power to throw off, or rid itself of refuse matter.

We have before seen that Magnetism and Electricity were among the primitive and essential developments of matter. We have also seen that Magnetism is a positive, and Electricity a negative agent; and that, as a necessary result of these, bodies were endowed with attractive and repulsive powers; hence, if, in the grand work of combination, any particles became negative to the mass, they would be repelled and sent off into the atmosphere, because of the attractive and repulsive powers exerted upon them by the various other forces in space, independent of the Sun; hence, there were continually being sent off from the Sun refuse particles, or particles negative to the mass, in concentric circles, which, in due time, were condensed, and formed into the planet termed Earth. The time, taken for the agglomeration of these particles into this formation, the human mind could not conceive, for *comparatively* it was an infinitude of time. The distance from the sun, of this mass (which was liquid, and attended by heat so intense that you could not conceive its intensity), gradually became greater as its particles increased in number — as by the attractive influence upon the particles of the sun, it was *continually* doing — and as its density increased.

The earth has holden many different relations to the sun, in different periods of its existence, proportioned to its density and attractive influence *for* the sun. This is evident from the fact, that the earth must have been — as it *was* — originally in a highly rarified state, and consequently would have retained a nearer distance to the sun under that condition, then when in a more dense state; because there would of necessity be a stronger influence exerted upon these particles by the sun, from the affinity between them, than by surrounding bodies. But when density increased, the attractive influence of the sun, and of other bodies, would be reduced to an equilibrium — which gradually occurred — and hence the earth would be located *by* the equilibrium of these forces.

The earth being established by these forces, the process of cooling, and of general development, commenced. Heat being impregnated with a disposition to fly from all heated bodies, in straight lines, by forces before mentioned, the process of cooling went *rapidly* on, though it would be needless for me to attempt to give you an idea of the length of time occupied therein — for, to your minds, it would be infinite. It followed, as a necessary consequence, that the external portion of the earth would cool with the greatest rapidity, and hence encrustation would ensue; and the *external*, or crust of the earth, being thus made dense, of course the internal would not be quenched, but pent up in a prison-house, molten and liquid; there were left undeveloped, beauty, life and power, that were destined to form no part of developed existence.

Thin crusts were formed over some portions of this immense mass of molten lava, while other parts refused to yield to the cooling influence for ages; but, when encrustation ensued over the whole earth, or a general coating was formed, these internal elements would break forth from their imprisonment, and pour out their melted masses upon the more quiet portions, so that for a long time *encrustation* was suspended or checked. Yet the laws, that were operating to prepare the mass, *would* not yield, but, after successive attempts, and incalculable periods, succeeded so far as to create so dense encrustation as to prevent these internal forces from destroying their labor. The elements within, raging, maniac-like, would throe and heave their mighty masses, as if to escape from their pent-up place; and hence mountains were thrown up here and there — valleys, as a necessary consequence, were formed, and the fair face of the universe was made distorted and uneven. The portions in which the crust was most thin were the scenes of the most *mighty* catastrophes; hence, as the earth cooled in different parts soonest, those in which cooling went on most rapidly were left most even. The atmosphere having been developed, these valleys became the theatres of mighty volumes of water, with the mountains for their banks, which they lashed with awful fury, so that, upon their going down, these huge piles presented ragged and awful aspects.

While cooling was taking place, the earth being prepared for the grand work of development, the elements were not idle, but, impregnated by electricity with a positive or negative state, the grand work of development and progression was going on. There was a grand war among the elements — a floating about of particles in search of kindred, that is incomprehensible: the whole mass was alive with agitation and motion. The first to assume form and shape were minerals. Particles would come together and unite themselves in eternal embraces, deposit themselves in their proper localities, and meet the contending forces as best they could.

The first formations were of granite rock, composed of mica, quartz, feldspar and hornblende (the last three most prominent), in a coarse, rough state, as granite now is. It must be remembered that this formation could not have happened until there had become a considerable coating upon the surface of the earth, when the internal heat, seeking vent, induced molecular substances to arise to the surface of the molten mass, where they aggregated, and formed this kind of rock, or the primary formation. This formation is an index of the elements, for there was then formed an atmosphere with a density corresponding to this formation, and as an ultimate of this a watery fluid, which we will term water. The atmosphere was then composed of different elements from now, as also was the water. Each formation had elements corresponding to its density and refinement. The atmosphere, at that time, was composed of a small portion of nitrogen, about one-fifth carbon and sulphuric acid, hydrogen and fluroine, oxygen. Water was composed of nitrogen, hydrogen, fluorine, oxygen and carbonic acid.

An almost endless period elapsed before the granite formation was completed, and other formations commenced. Frequent eruptions happened — mountains were thrown up, rocks ejected, valleys formed, and seas established. The valleys were made beds of seas — filled with the watery fluid of which I have before spoken — that went raging through them, with the mountain eminences for their banks, — which were much higher then than now, as those seas were oftentimes hundreds of miles in depth. Being dense, they lashed the mountain sides, ejected and wore away rocks, and carried the particles to their beds, all of which (assisted by the internal fires that were continually acting upon them) gave rise to the first stratified rock, gneiss and micaceous slate.

It may not be amiss for me here to state, that the spot upon which you are now sitting * was once the bed of a mighty sea, of many miles depth, with the Green mountains for its eastern, and the Adirondacks for its western bank; and hence the frequent occurrence of the slate formation in its original bed.

That the atmosphere and water were formerly much more dense than now, cannot be denied, as there can be found no one so blind, as not to see that all fluids must

* Rutland Co., Vt.

have been more gross, in their primitive states, than in their more progressed, or more fully developed stages, owing to the gross condition of matter, and the undeveloped and unsettled state of all substances. If physical proofs are necessary, the extremely superior power of water to wear away rocks, in its primitive states, than now, — as is evinced by the formation of the rocks to which I have referred, — is a sufficient proof.

The theory here advanced has been before the world, and was advanced by A. J. Davis, of whose philosophy allow me now to speak in commendable terms. In the main, the theories advanced by him are truthful and correct, and he placed before the world truths that were needed, and that, in more progressed periods of existence, will be duly appreciated.

The granite formation was the result of angular motion. It extends for many miles in depth, and as that formation is an index of developed elements, as air, water, &c., so the succeeding gneiss and slate formations indicate that these elements had refined, and attained a more perfect development; and had become so much perfected, that when, by the action of internal and external forces, the lower strata of the primary rocks were succeeded by the clay-slate and Grauwacke formations, animal and vegetable life were developed: from which fact, it is evident to your minds, that the state of these elements *may* be determined, during the processes, *by* the different formations. This formation is usually termed the transition from the primitive to the *fossiliferous*, as in it are found the remains of plants and animals in great variety, the *crinoides*, *conchiferæ crustacea*, *polypi* and *polyparia*. Had not these elements undergone a great change (as they are admitted to have done by men of science), neither animal nor vegetable life could have been sustained or generated.

It must not be supposed that these formations were the result of short periods of time; for, were I to attempt to impress upon you the length of time during which the Granite formation was being completed, and preparing for the *second* formation, you could not comprehend it. It was an infinitude of time; and this was equally the case with the transition and succeeding formations.

The elements being in an imperfect condition, it follows, as a necessary consequence, that vegetable and animal life were in an equally *imperfect* condition. The plants generated were flowerless and seedless, — hence had not the power of reproduction, which was equally the case with the animals.

Nature works by regular laws, and progression can only be attained by degrees, as perfection stamps no natural production in the outset, but is only arrived at by steady and gradual progression. As the mighty oak was once contained in the acorn, and obliged to pass through regular periods of germination and contention, before it attained its stately form and hardy powers, so all else in the universe came up by regular stages of gradation, from the first to the last, attaining new powers and perfection during each successive period, until comparative perfection stamps the whole natural kingdoms. Within the bosom of the Earth were contained embryo existences to infinity; yet those existences could not be brought forth in an hour, but must wait the slow progress of development. The elements must be reduced to their proper conditions — the *earth prepared* for their reception.

It must be remembered that an indefinite period elapsed between the slate and the succeeding carboniferous formation; and that, in the mean time, vegetables and animals had been developed to quite an extent. The elements had changed, and progression stamped *all* things. But before we notice, particularly, the carboniferous, or coal formation, it may be necessary for us to examine the condition of the earth, and also the developments, with some minuteness.

We have perceived that granite is composed of mica, hornblende, feldspar and quartz, and that the succeeding strata, or formations, were composed of disintegrated portions of rock, &c., gathered by the waters from the mountain sides. We have found that the micaceous-slate formation, by disintegration of its upper strata, was succeeded by the clay-slate, or fossiliferous formation, when we find lime generated in considerable quantities, the presence of which is evidenced by the appearance of shell-fish, whose shells were composed of lime.

We have also found that the air, as well as water, was impregnated with carbon in considerable quantities; and, at the period of which we now speak, the vegetable as well as animal kingdoms were, to quite an extent, developed. In various portions of the globe, trees had appeared, and various vegetables had gained a marked existence. At this period, too, the tides were raging with much fury, and changes were being rapidly made in the face of the universe. The waters had collected large quantities of shells and vegetables, which were conveyed to their beds, to unite with sedimentary particles of mica, carbon, lime, &c., and hence there commenced the carboniferous or coal era and formation. These vegetables, being acted upon by the water, from which they were continually receiving carbonized deposits, and also by the lime, which, in that period, was developed, were continually becoming carbonized, or formed into coal. That there were, at that period, trees of large dimensions, is evidenced from the remains of trees, at this day found in these formations, in a state of carbonization.

At the commencement of the carboniferous era the watery element had become so increased, that the former equilibrium was destroyed, and hence the internal fires must have vent, — during which period there was an upheaving of the chain of mountains in South America called the Andes, and the chain called the Apennines, in Spain. Various disturbances were occasioned thereby, of which I shall speak hereafter.

The tides at this time extended over a large portion of the Earth; hence the existence of fossils in crevices of mountains may be accounted for, as the deposits of this era.

The water was then, as well as the atmosphere, heavily impregnated with carbon, oxygen having been but partially developed. Of course no conflagration could ensue, which would have ensued had the air been possessed of its present quantity of that element. Of course animal life must become extinct in this era, as there was so much carbonic-acid gas in the air as to destroy it.

The action of the elements occasioned a union of lime and carbon, which, by coming together, became fused, and were deposited upon the slate formation in the form of carboniferous lime. By this union of carbon and lime, the elements were made less dense, and hence dry land became visible in many portions of the Earth. Upon the mountain eminences, thus left bare, vegetation sprang up with surprising avidity, and became exceedingly thrifty. Trees of immense size were formed, and so powerful became the growth, and so extensive, that the elements of the soil, necessary to support their life, were exhausted; and hence, in the process of ages, they decayed, became decomposed, and, by the avidity with which they took up carbon from the elements, were in the lapse of time formed into coal, and became one stratum of the carboniferous formation. Perhaps it is necessary that I should say that the tides washed these particles to their various beds.

This stratum was formed from the extreme avidity with which these bodies took up nitrogen and carbon from the air, together with metallic elements. This stratum was ages in being formed, and having been formed from the great reduction of the density of the elements, by the exhaustion of carbon, and consequently the generation of those elements that occasion and support vegetable life, another growth of trees was formed, which came up with even greater avidity than those which preceded them; and hence, in the course of time, reduced these elements again to such a point as to occasion the decay of these trees, and from them form another stratum. By this time the extra amount of carbon in the air, and other elements, was exhausted; and hence was established a period in creation, where vegetable and animal life could flourish. These strata of coal were frequently interspersed with strata of iron-stone, sandstone, and limestone.

This was a point, in the existence of the Universe, when the developments of elements were favored. A bright day dawned. The air became lively and exhilarating, from the oxygen with which it was impregnated in larger quantities than at any previous period. Water became more rare, and hence the great seas began to go down; vegetable and animal life were developed, and the grand work of perfection began under favorable auspices.

We have hastily passed over and examined the geological structure and condition of the Earth, up to the expiration of the carboniferous era, and it now behoves us to return, and in a more minute manner examine the various phenomena of stratification and formation.

We have found that the Primary formation is of granite rock, which is composed of aggregated particles, brought and *holden* together by chemical action, or by the power of heat and affinity. Granite is usually uniform in its combinations, being composed of mica, feldspar and quartz, with occasional garnets, hornblende and shorl. Being of the aggregate species, or species formed by the power of *chemical* action, it would naturally be more uniform in its elements than the cemented rocks, or those of the agglomerate species, which are of necessity multifarious in their combinations.

The granite formation plainly evinces that the original development of motion was the angular, as crystallization is most perfect in *this*, and less perfect in the succeeding formations, until it entirely disappears.

The granite formation originally extended, and now does extend around the globe. By the action of internal and external forces, it has been left uncovered and bare at the summits of your highest mountains, and oftentimes in your valleys. This rock forms the base of the mountains of Switzerland, as also of the Alps generally. There are various strata of intervening rocks of different elements upon this formation, the first of which is gneiss, which forms the larger portion of the Carpathian mountains. The *level* of *gneiss* is lower than that of granite, mica-slate lower than that of gneiss, and the clay-slate lowest of all. There are intermediate strata of porphyry, sienite, serpentine, and strown throughout the mass, as 't were by some careless hand, are topaz, quartz, serpentine, porphyry, trap, gypsum, flint-slate and limestone.

We may notice here, that, from the granite to the transition or Grauwacke system, there were no traces of any carboniferous substances, or of life of any kind; hence the inevitable conclusion that for the whole space of time occupied in the development of the granite and gneiss formation, carbon was not developed, at least to any great extent; and hence animal or vegetable life did not, nor could exist in those periods.

We have before seen that, during the process of making up the granite formation, an atmosphere was developed, mountains formed, and seas established. We have also found that water was then an exceedingly dense body, and possessed of much greater power to wear away solid substances than now; — hence upon the granite formation was established the secondary formation, or stratified rock. The seas, lashing the sides of their banks, wore away the rocks, which we have found to be composed of mica, feldspar, and hornblende, and conveyed them to their beds, where, being subjected to the action of the water, as also the heat of the internal fires that were continually seeking vent, they were formed into gneiss and micaceous slate; which, in their turns, became the beds of porphyry, quartz, feldspar, serpentine, topaz, trap, gypsum, flint-slate, sienite and limestone, interspersed with layers of slate; — hence here you find, in the second formation, the first stratified rocks, which were distributed in layers one above the other, in regular succession, gneiss being lowest, micaceous slate next, and sienite last. It must be remembered that these different strata were many ages in being formed; hence each successive stratum would be of a different order, because this formation, being the result of chemical action, of course the particles in sediment, during each formation, would be acted upon differently; hence the difference in the combinations.

The upper strata of the gneiss formation having become disintegrated by the action of internal and external forces, it was succeeded by the transition, or Grauwacke system. The appearance of this system evinces a change in the elements, as by fossils of ferns, palms, pines and moss, as also crustaceous animals, it is proven that the Earth had become capable of generating life, which, during previous formations, it had not done. I have before said that *life* generated at this period, both *animal* and vegetable, was of an imperfect order, as the powers of reproduction were not possessed; which shows that, although there was then existing the power to *generate* life, there was not the power to *support* it to any considerable extent.

At this period the atmosphere, as well as water, must have become less dense than previously, and hence the particles expanded, and the equilibrium formerly holden was destroyed. The circumference of the Earth had changed very considerably, and, to restore the broken equilibrium, various mountains were thrown up.

Carbon had now become developed in considerable quantities, and began to pervade the whole Universe. Large quantities of carbonic-acid gas were generated, and hence a destruction of life ensued, and the transition or Grauwacke formation became the seat of carboniferous lime and coal.

The density of the Earth having increased, of course its motion upon its axis increased also, and hence the tides began to extend over the Earth. These gathered up shells and vegetable remains, which were wafted to the tops of the highest mountains even, and hence the fissures that existed in their sides became the seat of various carboniferous, quartaceous, micaceous and other matter, — which would result as a natural consequence from the fusion created by the union of carbon and lime. A stratum of carboniferous lime was formed, and hence the atmosphere and water, having become somewhat relieved of this cumbrous substance, became less dense, and dry land became visible. Mountain tops peered out above the watery masses, and being extremely fertile, trees sprang up and grew with astonishing rapidity and thickness, until the elements of the soil, necessary for their support, had become exhausted, when, as a natural result, decay and decomposition would follow.

Deposits of iron-stone, lime-stone, green-stone, and amygdaloid, had been made upon the Grauwacke system, and these decomposed particles of trees being acted upon by the water and atmosphere, and having a stronger attraction for carbon (which they took up with avidity), nitrogen and metallic substances, than for oxygen, which at this period had been but slightly developed, the first deposit of *coal* was made. This stratum was ages in being formed.

The atmosphere became much less dense from this exhaustion of carbon by these substances, and hence, in the course of ages, there sprang up another growth of trees, which grew even with greater rapidity than their predecessors, and hence, in due time also, exhausted the elements necessary for their support,—which were but imperfectly developed,—and hence in due time also decayed, became decomposed, and formed another stratum of coal. In the coal formation there frequently occur beds of tin, iron, lead, limestone, &c.

The carbon having been absorbed from the atmosphere, its density was decreased, and the equilibrium between the internal and external forces was destroyed. The molten masses in the bowels of the Earth, no longer sufficiently restrained, expanded, and sought vent. The face of the Universe was sadly changed. Mountains were moved from their places, strata were broken up, and rocks and minerals were thrown from the lower strata to the surface of the Earth. Volcanoes vomited forth their lava, and mountains were permanently established. It was during this commotion that the Alps were established, and hence their granite base. The Carpathian mountains were also thrown up, new valleys were formed, and seas located.

For a long time the Universe wore a sad aspect. The labor of ages seemed upon the verge of destruction; but in the progress of time the atmosphere gained force from the internal elements, and the raging masses within retired quietly to their former passivity. During this catastrophic period, huge rocks were split asunder and parted forever by the ingress of other substances. And immediately following this convulsion of elements, the crust of the Earth sank, and the elements were reörganized.

It will at once appear evident to your minds that this last mentioned era in the work of formation was absolutely necessary for the attainment of the great aim of matter. Had not the atmosphere been relieved of the carbonic-acid gas, with which, at the expiration of the Grauwacke system, it was impregnated animal life could never have been supported or generated; and hence the Earth, at this day, would have been a wild waste of useless matter, containing within itself, in embryo, the same powers, energies and beauties, that at this moment exist in *development.* The busy hordes of human beings, who, at this day, are laboring to *perfect* and beautify the Universe, would have slumbered in undeveloped quietude in the desolate waste of matter.

But this era occurred, and by no possibility could it be prevented from occurring. There were laws governing matter, forces urging it on, whose progressive power and influences *must* be obeyed. The work of development could not be checked;—hence you see the truth of the proposition, before advanced by me, that matter is progressive, and has within itself the power to produce its ultimates. But you must not suppose that those ultimates were even at this period attained, for the grand work of development was but upon the *threshold* of progression;—there were yet other innumerable ages to roll away, before those ultimates could be attained.

What endless beauties round you are displayed,—
How shines the *Godhead* in the *darkest* shade!

The carboniferous era passed away; the black masses of coal and minerals, that therein were developed, began to be hidden by deposits from the atmosphere, &c. Vegetation sprang up, and animal life began again to exist. The waters had become reduced to nearly their present elements, and oxygen and nitrogen were the predominant elements of the air. The carbon from the air having been nearly exhausted, the coal era must close,—otherwise these deposits would have continued to be made, even to this day, and to all eternity. Evaporation commenced with great vigor, and hence frequent rains, oftentimes lasting for many days, incessantly occurred. Various gases had been generated, and, by the force of *all* these powers, there were made extensive deposits of disintegrated rocks, matter from the atmosphere, &c., upon the coal formation. Decay attended the vegetable as well as animal kingdom, and hence their decomposed elements were also used in the general coating of the Earth. These deposits, called alluvial deposits, are made even at this day.

Nature was struggling to prepare the Earth for the development of its highest existence, "Man," and she labored with assiduity for many ages, after the carboniferous era had passed away, before it was deemed fit to be "man's dwelling-place." The internal elements were continually seeking vent, and new gases being developed, which, uniting with the various substances on the surface of the Earth, formed a new stratification. From the extreme avidity with which limestone took up carbon and metallic substances, the chalk formation was originated,—various oxydes were formed, &c.

It is a well established fact, among chemists, that there are fifty-five elements which enter into and compose the various substances in existence; and, furthermore, that these elements unite differently under different action, affinities, &c., and hence give rise to *various* substances. Therefore limestone, being acted upon by the gases, developed after the coal formation was established, was converted into chalk, which, in its turn, became the seat of the oolite formation; which in *its* turn, became the seat of *lias;* and, throughout these formations, are to be found several kinds of metals, as iron, lead, copper, &c. Limestone took up large quantities of carbon, and having an affinity for metallic substances, which it took up, crystallized, and gave rise to the chalk formation.

Above the coal, during the era of which we now speak, was formed the new red sand-stone system, composed of an aggregate of particles which were afloat in the atmosphere, water, &c.; which formation produced a change in the elements, so far as to reduce the density of the air and water; and thus must happen another of those catastrophes that marked the close of the carboniferous era. The external pressure having been reduced very considerably by an exhaustion of the carbon, &c., in them, the equilibrium formerly holden between the external and internal elements was destroyed, and the internal elements again raged and sought an opportunity to escape. There was a long night of convulsions; volcanoes vomited forth their fires, strata were broken and thrown up, mountains were formed, and islands disgorged in the seas. This convulsion was felt most forcibly at the poles, and south of the equator.

It was during this era that many of the South-sea islands were thrown up; and I may here state that very many of the islands in existence are merely the works of various little insects, that have aggregated in masses, and established what are termed coral reefs, islands, &c. These *infusoria* are so minute as to be imperceptible to the eye. Three hundred of them would hardly fill the space of a square inch.

During this mighty convulsion, seas were thrown up from their usual beds, and their waters sent over a large portion of the Earth. Rivers were turned from their channels, and lakes driven to other valleys. Various shells, vegetable and animal remains, were scattered over the Earth by the waters, which, from the force of the internal fires, gases, &c., aggregated, and gave rise to what is termed the Oolite formation.

After a long period of raging and warring between

the internal and external elements, an equilibrium was established, and the density of the air and water was greatly reduced. The atmosphere had become so refined and rare as to admit the light of the sun freely, and hence there arose upon the face of the earth a bright morning, wherein might be generated and supported a higher order of animal and vegetable life. Evaporation took place with greater force than ever before, and hence, from the ocean and other watery reservoirs, were sent off large quantities of water, which were swept over the earth, and descended upon the mountains and valleys in the form of rains, &c., which dashed down their sides in torrents, washing away rocks, &c., with rapidity and ease, whose disintegrated particles were carried by the waters into the valleys, there to form various substances.

These substances were formed and scattered over the different formations just in proportion to the nature of the particles in sediment. If disintegrated particles of quartz impregnated the waters, they were brought together and aggregated in the form of crystals, agate, cornelian, &c. If the water was impregnated with limestone, the aggregation of the particles produced alabaster, marble, &c.; hence the reason why, in various formations, there are found various depositions of limestone, marble, and kindred substances. Some mountains were covered with quartz, others with limestone, &c., which rocks being worn away by the waters, and their disintegrated particles swept into the valleys, would be united, by the laws of affinity, and thus give rise to the various interspersions.

It is a fact, well ascertained by scientific men, that

the surface of the earth is composed of various oxydes, which, when fused, give rise to metallic substances, as iron, tin, copper, silver, gold, &c.; hence, the inference to be drawn from the existence of these metals, in various formations, is, that the oxydes, from which they were developed, were subjected to fusion by the internal fires of the earth, and thus were these various ores and metallic substances produced. Various portions of the matter, held in sediment by the waters, were brought together in the form of paste, and hence various rocks were formed,—solid and hard,—which are endless in variety, and many of which are nameless.

We have found that, during this period, there were frequent rains, high winds, &c., which lasted many days in succession. The waters of the seas, lakes, rivers, &c., held in sediment much loose matter that was destined to assist in the grand work of preparing the earth for the abiding place of man. The waters evaporated, and being swept by the winds over the earth, descended in the form of rains, that, in comparison to the rains witnessed by you at this day, might be called torrents. These rains and winds often produced at the poles *immense* icebergs,—much more extensive than now,—which, by a succession of winters, were continually increased in bulk, until they had accumulated a world of water.

A succession of warm summers, produced by the perpendicularity of the earth's axis to the plane of the ecliptic (which, at this period, was occasioned by forces of which I shall hereafter speak), succeeded in melting away these huge mountains of ice, which were carried, by force of rains and winds, to various portions of the earth, where they were melted, and so great was their volume, that a grand inundation of the earth followed. Nearly the whole earth was submerged, animal and vegetable life yielded to its ravages, and in many parts were destroyed. Human life was at that period extant, and a large portion of human existence was swept away:—hence the legend of the Flood, and hence the diluvial deposits. After the waters had raged from point to point, they were obliged to seek an equilibrium, and, retiring to the valleys, various oceans, seas, lakes and rivers, were formed.

This Deluge *must of necessity* happen, and was not sent, as many at this day suppose, and as the Bible alleges, to destroy the wicked from the face of the earth. Laws had been established, that must be obeyed, among which were several to produce this submersion.

The force of capillary attraction, aided and assisted by heavy rains, extreme cold, and strong winds, would necessarily produce icebergs. The relative change in the density of the earth, and the consequent change in the influence of other bodies upon it, would alter the relative situation of the earth to the sun, and hence change the seasons; and heat, having power to melt away ice. it necessarily followed that the change in the seasons, occasioned by the change in the earth's situation,—the perpendicularity of its axis to the plane of the ecliptic,—would increase the length of summers, intensity of heat, &c.; and, assisted by rains and winds, these forces would produce a melting away and removal of the large icebergs accumulated at the poles; and the melting away of the icebergs would destroy the equilibrium formerly holden by the waters of the earth, occasion seas to overleap their boundaries, rivers and lakes to forget their channels, and a grand submersion to follow.

It must not be supposed that the whole earth was submerged, for there was never a sufficient quantity of water upen the earth to produce a universal deluge; and this leads me to speak of the absurdity of the scriptural account of the Flood.

It is said in the Bible, and believed by a large class of men, that mankind had become so prone to evil, committed so great wickednesses, that God determined to destroy them from the face of the earth, in order that a new race might spring up, which would better adorn the universe, and worship him; consequently he came in a vision to a man called Noah, and advised him of his intentions, telling him that it was his pleasure that he and his family should escape the general inundation, and, to this end, he must build himself an ark of Gopher wood, three hundred cubits in length, fifty cubits in breath, and thirty cubits in height, in which he was to make rooms, *pitched* over to prevent the ingress of water, and in these were to be deposited, of each of the animals of the field, to restock the earth, birds of the air, [fishes of the sea,*] and all creeping things—some by pairs and some by sevens.

Noah built the ark as directed, and the Lord came to him in another vision and advised him of the day when he should be prepared. Consequently the doors of the ark were opened, and there were gathered together into that ark two of each of the animals of the

* It was remarked, in explanation, that "all flesh" must include the *fishes of the sea*—else they, too, would have been *drowned!*

field, birds of the air, [fishes of the sea,] and all creeping things, and such as crawl upon the belly, some by pairs and some by sevens.

When this august body had become located in their respective apartments, Noah and his family went in—the doors were closed, the windows of the heavens were opened, and incessantly, for forty days and forty nights, the rain descended in torrents, until the peaks of the highest mountains were lost in the bosom of the waters, and all mankind, &c., were swept away, from the stage of life and activity, to that lake burning with fire and brimstone, prepared for the Devil and his angels!

That must have been a pleasing spectacle for God. No doubt he sat above the waters, *Nero-like*, laughing at and gloating over the miseries of mankind, whom he had created and pronounced *Good*—but afterwards "repented of having created." I say there is *no doubt* he did this, if he really sent the flood, as alleged in the Holy Writ. But I will now say that God never yet sent his flood to destroy mankind;—and, whenever any calamity, among the elements, has occurred, to sweep away any portion of life—either human or other—it has occurred by force of necessity, of natural laws, whose progress even Deity had not the power to stay.

Let us now examine into the probability of the truth of the scriptural account of the flood. In the first place, let us inquire whether God, according to the Scripture itself, profited at all by, or in the remotest degree attained the end, for which it is alleged he sent the aforesaid flood.

It is said that he repented that he had made man, because of their wickedness, and hence determined to destroy all but Noah and his family, whom he saved for restocking the Earth with a more moral and God-loving people.

Let us also premise from the Bible that God is an infinite personage, and knew from the beginning all which was to occur in the future, even unto the end of time;—consequently he must have known, when he created man, every act that he was to perform on Earth; he must have known that their wickedness would be as it was. And now, in view of this, let me ask, is it not strange, *exceedingly* strange, that he should have created man? Does any one entertain so poor an opinion of God, as to suppose that he would have created him merely for the purpose of destroying him? Yet, if you believe the scriptural account of the deluge, you must certainly conclude that God *delighted* in the destruction of his children; that he *created* them for the purpose of destroying them,—else why did he create them, when he knew from the beginning that he was *to* destroy them?

Reader, do not be astonished that I deal thus with the Bible, for I do it simply to show you its absurdities, as well as the absurd notions that people entertain of God.

Now it seems to me that if God is, and was the all-powerful being that he is represented to be, he might have avoided this mighty catastrophe. If he had the power to create man, to destroy him, he had equally the power to *control* him; and it seems strange to me, according to the account, that he did not, instead of destroying man exert his power to change his conduct, to control his life,—which he could easily do.—and thus avoid the necessity of repenting that he had made man. But, in view of *all* things, it seems stranger to me that God should have allowed any to escape death, when it appears to have been his intention to build up or produce a more moral and God-loving people by the flood. It was as easy for him to *recreate* man, as to *destroy* him. Hence, it seems to me, that if he sent the flood for the purpose alleged, he was extremely destitute of foresight, for by the Bible itself you are taught that no sooner had Noah got out of the ark, than he planted himself a vineyard and became drunk with wine,—in which situation being found by one of his sons, who exposed his shame and mocked him (Ham), he was cursed, and sent out upon the face of the Earth to be the root of a stock of negroes. The sons of Noah began to multiply, and became in a short space of time more wicked even than those who had preceded them.

Now is it not a disparagement of the wisdom of God to suppose that he would send his flood to destroy mankind, because of their wickedness, and suffer to escape a family that was to be the founder of a far *more* wicked race?

Again; it is a great query with me whence a sufficient quantity of water could be obtained to deluge the whole Earth to the extent it is there alleged occurred. It seems that the flood descended in the form of rain. Rains are occasioned by an evaporation of water, from the waters of the Earth,—the vapor being swept away to various localities, to descend in showers, storms, &c. Now it seems to me that,—rains always occurring in this way,—if the waters had descended for the space of forty days and nights, instead of inundating the whole Earth, they would have sought their channels again, and, by the time these were filled, that the rains must have ceased.

It is said that God became sorry that he had done as he did, and consequently entered into and formed a covenant with Noah, that he would never destroy the Earth by flood again, and, as a seal of this important obligation, placed his Bow in the heavens.

Now it strikes me, that, whenever there is moisture in the form of rain-drops in the atmosphere, and sunlight to fall upon them, as a necessary result, rainbows, as they are familiarly called, would ensue. They happen by force of a law that existed innately in matter, and, long before the aforesaid flood happened, were set in the sky.

Another very strange query will present itself to your minds, and that is, how there could have been crammed into that little ark, covering but a few thousand square feet, so many animals.

At that period, it is plainly proven, by fossil remains, that there were in existence animals far more huge in dimensions than now, — two of which would fill a small ark; — yet, according to scripture, two Mammoths, two Elephants, two Whales, two Rhinoceroses, two Sea-Serpents, two Sharks, two Apes, two Kangaroos, two Orang-Outangs, two Monkeys, two Rattlesnakes, two Crocodiles, two Alligators, two Lions, two Bears, &c., &c., &c., almost to infinity, were stored away in a little building not an acre square. It is a great wonder how there could have been enough air for all this *happy*, lucky lot, — and what they ate. It is also difficult to imagine how the whales and fishes lived without water.

But I will not go on with this disgusting rehearsal. Common sense *revolts at such stuff*, and the day is not distant when these absurd and ridiculous accounts will be committed to the shades of oblivion, where they properly belong, and mankind be led by the dictates of reason and truth.

The rack, the inquisition, the scaffold, and stake, originally were used as a *quietus* to the advance of science, but the days of religious intolerance and persecution have gone by; the light of science *will* stream in upon the world; and hence you find men endeavoring to distort the Bible into such shapes as to obscure its imperfections exposed by science; — but their screens are flimsy, and but a few short seasons will roll away, when that book will be regarded as it is, much of it, simply a mass of legendary tales. But I will return to my subject.

The waters sent over the Earth, by the melting away of the icebergs, contained in sediment much matter, which was deposited, together with other matter, accumulated in its ragings from mountains, &c., upon the Earth, which deposits are now called the diluvial formation. The raging of the waters was terrible. Mountains, that towered towards the heavens in princely grandeur, were reduced to little hills. Hills were converted into mountains. Seas changed their beds, rivers sought new channels, and a wide change was effected in the face of the universe.

It must be remembered that the whole Earth was not inundated, but the eastern continent was chiefly the seat of this convulsion of waters.

By the melting away of these stupendous icebergs

the equilibrium between the internal and external forces was again destroyed. Volcanoes sent forth their fires. Islands were thrown up, and rain, smoke and lava descended upon the Earth in torrents, laying waste to a vast deal of human life. In the short space of five days the equilibrium was reëstablished, the waters sought their beds, and Nature began to put forth her energies to repair the injuries done to the face of creation.

We have before observed that human life was at this time developed, and hence each nation and tribe has its legend of the flood, all of which differ, and all of which are equally incorrect.

Various strata were formed by this convulsion, of which it is not my province to speak.

We have, in a brief manner, traced matter from its primitive condition up to the development of the climax of Nature's efforts. We have seen the Earth laboring to fit itself for man's abiding place, and have found her labors crowned with success; and it now behoves us to return, and in a brief manner trace her progress in developing life, and its ultimate, Man.

CHAPTER V.

MAN.

I HAVE hastily sketched the progress of matter from its original chaotic state to that point in time when the Earth became prepared for the generation and support of animal life. In the hasty sketch drawn, I have sufficiently illustrated the truth of the proposition, laid down in that preceding chapter, that "matter is progressive, and has within itself the power to produce its ultimates."

You have seen the wild chaos of matter so far turned into subjection to natural laws, as to give rise to the first, or granite formation. You have seen this formation close, to give rise to another, the gneiss formation; and this, in its turn, succeeded by the *transition*, the transition by the coal, and the coal by various strata, all of which have given rise to various states of atmosphere, &c.

In that rapid sketch, you have seen the work of development going on from point to point, and have seen that each formation has been an ascending and necessary step in the ladder of progression. You have seen the first point in time when life was developed, and that *the* life developed has invariably been analogous to the state of matter, the elements, &c.; that, as matter refined or progressed, life of all kinds progressed and perfected itself; that all the great convulsions in nature have had their due influence in the work of development, and have been necessary consequences of natural laws. You have seen nature untiringly, assiduously laboring with the elements, to prepare the Earth for a grand end. Your own perceptions will lead you to the inference that that end was the creation of Man.

I shall not go back to trace the progress of animal life from its development to its ultimate, as that will be unnecessary; for, the enlightened mind, from what has already been written, will concede that "matter is progressive," and that life of all kinds is progressive, varying, as I have before said, as the elements are changed in their character. It is enough for me to say that "Man," the masterpiece of nature's productions, the highest exhibition of superior skill, came up, by regular stages of gradation, from the lowest point of animal life, to his present high state. It will be unnecessary for me to point out the connecting links 'twixt him and the monad, for the veriest school-boy is familiar with them. I will simply state that man *came* up by regular stages of gradation from the monad.

The ultimate of matter is not met in man's earthly existence; for he has within himself a progressive principle, or spirit, that is developed in the body, thrown off at death, and commences a still higher state of life in celestial regions. Man is truly a superior being, because the highest physical development of matter. He contains within himself a principle of intelligence, that is possessed by none other of the animal kingdom. Before I speak further of man, allow me to notice the scriptural account of his creation.

The ancients, who were fruitful in expedients, deemed it necessary to account for the creation of man; hence, after preparing the Earth for his reception, in a very summary manner, they proceed to tell you, that upon the sixth day of creation, God created man after his own image, and breathed into his nostrils the breath of life. But, in the hurry of creation, he forgot to make a woman, and hence he had to place Adam in a deep sleep, that he might take out a few of his left ribs to create Eve, a female.

Now it has always puzzled me, and I presume that it has likewise troubled yourselves, to imagine how God could make a woman from a few of Adam's ribs; and still more it perplexes me to imagine the reason or necessity for so doing, unless he had used up all the flesh-material in making Adam.

It seems that when Adam awoke, he found his ribs gone, and, in looking about to find them, discovered that they had been formed into a pretty "Eve."

God placed this happy pair in the Garden of Eden, and left them to be as happy as needs be. But, wishing to try the power of his last handiwork to resist temptation, it seems he forbid their tasting the fruit of a particular tree, under the penalty of certain death, should they do so; and, to make the temptation still stronger, he created and placed in the Garden a serpent, whose duty it was *to beguile* the woman, if possible, and get her to taste the fruit, — well knowing that though the *serpent* might not be able to seduce Adam, *Eve* could.

It seems that, after a long series of temptings, Eve was induced to take of the fruit of the forbidden tree, and Adam partook also from the hand of Eve. God all the while had been concealed in ambush; but, as soon as he found his law had been broken, and the fruit tasted, he came forth, and poured his wrath both upon the pair and the serpent. Adam and Eve were driven from the Garden, and Sin was ushered into the world. The poor serpent, who had no more than done his duty, was cursed, made to crawl on his belly, and to have his head bruised by the seed of the woman. God then swore in his wrath that "Death" should happen, &c.

Now this account of creation, the fall, &c., does not contemplate a very high state for mankind; because it would seem from it that God originally did not provide a haven for the weary soul, when the cares of earth were strong, but intended that he should multiply to a certain extent, and then cease to multiply, and live in the body forever. Let us examine this account somewhat, and find what ridiculous notions people will hug to their hearts, and cling to, even in an enlightened age of the world.

Reader, what idea have you of God? Do you regard him as an all-wise and powerful being? Do you regard him as a *humane* FATHER, or as a *barbarous monster?* If you regard him as a humane being, and a being of infinite power, can you for a moment believe that he created man in the manner represented in Holy Writ,—subjected him to temptations, caused his fall, cursed him forever, and introduced sin into the world? Is such a series of acts compatible with the nature of an all-wise and perfect being? *No, no;* human reason revolts at such ideas, and it is only a *mental passiveness* that allows any one to credit such narrations. Should the mind be allowed to be *passive* upon Divine matters? For what purpose were your reasoning faculties given you? Was it not that you might be able to detect right and wrong? By what are you to determine whether the Bible is the word of God? Are you not to be allowed to subject it to the test of your reason? How else can you determine its genuineness? Will it not stand the test of human reason? If not, it should most certainly not be credited. Let priests tell you, as much as they please, that the ways of God are above human comprehension,—your own common sense teaches you that you have a right to think and to reason upon matters within the scope of human thought.

One exceedingly important fact escaped the notice of the writer of Genesis. It is a well ascertained fact—and is said in a subsequent chapter of the Bible—that there *were* giants in those days, in the land, and long before Adam was created. Now giants are embraced in the category of human beings, and must have been possessed of human faculties. When were *they* created?

Let the mind, for one single hour, scan the records of the *soi-disant* Holy Writ, and it will revolt at its absurdity. I am confident that pious eyes will turn in holy horror from these pages, but I am speaking *Truth*—if not, let him who *can*, contradict it.

Man was developed as the highest physical ultimate of matter, and endowed with a progressive spirit, that cannot and will not be chained. Error may for a time dampen its energies, and stay its progress, assisted by the machinations of persecution, but it will ultimately burst its fetters, cast aside its chains, and seek after and find truth. The intelligent mind will not be satisfied with mere ambiguous legends, and wild creations of fancy, but will search for a better base upon which to found its religion.

Man, having come up by regular stages of gradation from the monad, has within himself the types of all existences, and a combination of all motions, hence is superior to all other of the animal creation.

I may here briefly state, in substantiation of the proposition before laid down, in reference to the development of man, that fossil remains, found in the different formations, plainly show that matter had within itself powers to generate animal life in a perfect or imperfect state, in proportion to its own perfect or imperfect condition. In the Transition formation, you will find the crustaceous animals developed, and, in time, this succeeded by the fish, this running into the saurian, the saurian into the bird, the bird into the marsupial, the marsupial into the mammalial, the mammalial into the human;—and thus, by regular improvements upon life, during distinct periods, was man developed.

The fact, that, during the first era of life, fishes were developed, and next the saurian, having all the attributes of the fish, and more, &c., &c., is sufficient to satisfy any one that man is the ultimate of Nature's efforts, and that, as an end, each animal development was unfolded and became continually improved, as the condition of matter improved, until man capped the climax of life.

Reason is alone possessed by man. All other of the animal kingdom exhibit intelligence of a peculiar kind, but he alone, of all the rest, exhibits and possesses a progressive tendency.

The robin builds its nest in the same form, and ushers in the rising day with the *same* tune that it sang upon the first morn of creation. The beaver constructs its dam, and builds it habitation after the same fashion that its progenitors did; and thus, all through the animal kingdom, you find a *fixed* principle governing each class, a principle from which there is no progression or retrocession, but a *fixedness* of habit that was the same yesterday, to-day, and will be the same forever.

This is instinct;—but *man*, from the first hour of his

development, has gone on in the path of progression, continually changing his mode of life, devising new means, attaining new ends, until the face of the universe is covered with specimens of his genius and skill. Not satisfied with the present, he is continually inventing new things, discovering and applying new principles, until his power seems God-like. Not satisfied with a knowledge of the little, pent-up world which is the theatre of his life, he has roved among the stars, mapped down their localities, noted their revolutions, fancied their internal condition, until they have become "milestones in a familiar path." From all other of the animal kingdom he is distinguished by this *progressive* spirit, and *this* is the result of *reason.*

If the young robin be removed from its kind, untutored and untaught in the architecture of its species, it will build its nest as well, and in the same form, as when surrounded by its kindred. But remove a child from its parents, and place it in the wilds of the forest, and though it will seek for itself a shelter from the storms, build itself a home,. and exhibit superior powers to the mere *animals* about it, it will not exhibit the skill and refinement of its species; because the innate principles of nature have not been developed by the power of discipline and education. Yet allow this child the power to propagate, and found a new race, and soon the powers of the mind will begin to exhibit themselves in various improvements, until, *perhaps*, that newly founded race will outstrip its progenitors in skill and knowledge. Thus it will be perceived that man is truly a progressive being. Created and endowed with superior powers, he evidently has a high mission to perform, and it behoves you to pause upon the threshold of life, and endeavor to discern what that mission is. He has physical wants to supply,—he must have a shelter from the storms, raiment to protect him from the inclemencies of the weather, and food to supply the demands of Nature ; but to supply these wants is not the sole *object* in his creation; for, if it was, then is he merely a *physical* being and an *animal*.

Man has other and higher duties to perform, besides these, for he is a *spiritual* as well as physical creature. He is a part and parcel of that superior intelligence, who was the architect of the universe. But it is a lamentable fact that at this day men forget the *true* aims of life, and make their sole object wealth. They bow devoutly at the shrine of Mammon, and worship no other God. A man is measured by the amount of *gold* he has, and not by his intellectual and moral worth.

The first aspiration breathed into the mind of the child from the cradle is to gain *gold*. He is taught by his ambitious parents that all other aims are merely minor objects, and must be sunk in this. The priest goes into his pulpit and preaches—not for the glory of God, or the spiritual elevation of his church. He caters to the views and inclinations of the church, because he fears to lose his *support* by doing otherwise. *Interest* requires that he should be a *hypocrite*, and he bows to its requirement. And, in fact, throughout every department of life, you find the same power operating. But few *dare* take an independent stand, lest they shall lose pecuniarily, and be subjected to popular persecution. Thank Heaven, there are a few *bold* minds, that, reckless of pecuniary interest or popular favor, dare be

MEN. It is this same *interest* of which I have spoken that has kept the religion of the day alive, that has shielded the Bible from its proper fate, and preserved error.

Man is not simply a *physical* being, hence his aims should not be solely physical. It is his highest duty to develop and unfold the intellectual powers that Nature has lavished upon him—to cultivate and refine his spiritual part, by a study of Nature and her laws; for by so doing, alone, can be obtained the *true* end of his existence. To live in harmony with Nature, one must needs be acquainted with her manifold laws, and to be acquainted with these laws he must study them.

The ultimate of matter is not met with in man's bodily life:—he is placed on Earth to develop, unfold, enlarge the spiritual principle which he contains, that he may be prepared to take a proper stand in celestial regions. For, as the spirit is developed, enlarged *in* the body, will it be prepared to take a higher or lower stand *in* those regions. Man is a progressive being; his progression, commencing on Earth, is continued forever in the Spirit Land. Hence it behoves all to take proper care that their spiritual welfare be attended to—that their spiritual powers be developed and cultivated. Let *gold*, fame, every worldly ambition, instead of being *prime*, be the minor objects of life, and your spiritual progression your absorbing aim; then, and not till then, will society be reduced to its proper condition, and a grand harmonial system be established on Earth.

Society exists upon a wrong basis, and, as the chief cause of this inharmonious condition, I may mention the Religious Dogmas of the day. I always said, when on earth, and I now repeat, that enlightened minds can never *honestly* entertain the ridiculous ideas advanced by the religionists of the day, or accredit the Bible as the word of God; but that the tendency of these is to produce hypocrites and infidels. From the absurdities that the mind discerns in the dogmas of the Church, and in the Holy Writ, which they are simply *passive* to, mankind come to doubt the existence of *God* even, and hence make the aims of life purely *physical.* This is the natural result of absurd religion; and this is the condition of society to-day, and such will continue to be the state of society until *religion* is based upon reason and common sense — until the laws of Nature are appreciated and understood.

The tendency of the religion of the day is not *moral* — as the condition of society plainly evinces. God is not worshipped in your churches, but is mocked, blasphemed by hypocrites and knaves. I say that the religion of the day is *demoralizing*, and crushes beneath its demonish feet the noblest attributes of the soul, blasts its *natural* aspirations, and feeds it on "air;" and I need but refer to the present moral condition of society to substantiate this proposition. Your priests claim to be *spiritual* teachers, and to them are you called for spiritual knowledge. Let us see if they are what they claim to be.

The "orthodox" portion of the world claim, as an axiom, that the Bible is the word of God. That the fall of man brought sin, and all its dire effects into the world, and made it necessary for God to create a Heaven and a Hell, — Heaven to be the abode of those who led righteous lives, and found favor in his eyes — Hell to be the abode of the wicked, and the kingdom of the devil. Finding that a large class of his children were getting into hell, he deemed it expedient to send his son into the world to be persecuted and crucified, that man, through him, might be saved from his sins by repentance.

Christ being crucified, however, by the people, a double burthen was placed upon the poor sinner; for not only is he now obliged to atone for his own sins, but also for the sins of his forefathers, — a sort of attainting system, that exists in some nations now, by which the children are obliged to bear the sins of their fathers.

Priests tell you that Christ was sent into the world to be a mediator between God and man; — hence, if you will but *repent* of your sins, even though an hour, or a moment before death, they will be forgiven, and you can be ushered into the joys of Heaven. Thus the veriest villains on Earth — murderers, thieves, liars, &c. — can continue their evil career through a long course of life, and if, upon their death-beds, they see fit to repent of their sins, they will be forgiven, washed away by the blood of the Lamb, and their miserable souls, will be ushered immaculate into the presence of God, to be the companions of saints and angels. By a few words whispered in the ear of a priest, they are saved from the pangs of hell.

Now what is the effect of such a religion? I hardly need answer. What an idea of God must men have, who can credit such stuff! How elevated their notions of life and its ends! What an incentive to *intellectual* and *moral* progression! Beware of so dangerous notions, for I can assure you, and your own reason will *re*ässure you that they are false, absurd, *dangerous*. They leave entirely out of view the progressive nature of man, and make him a mere pantomime. They give to God qualities such as are despisable in man, and much more despisable in a superior being. If all that is necessary for the washing away of sin is simply a falling upon the knees, and saying "Glory to God," a few moments before physical dissolution, then God is a vain, boastful God, and man a mere sycophant, — created by God simply that his vanity might be gratified by hypocritical and fawning tongues; — and it matters but little what attention is paid to the development and cultivation of the attributes of the soul, — for they will be of no avail, save only as they conduce to worldly comfort and profit. Intellectual and moral improvement is entirely useless, further than the simple attainment of physical ends. How ridiculous!

That the above inferences may properly be drawn from the creeds of the churches of the day will appear evident from the idea entertained of Heaven by religionists generally. You are told in your churches that Heaven is a land afar off in the regions of space, where the weary soul is refreshed from the cares of Earth by the splendor and glory about it. You are told that it is a large city, called New Jerusalem, whose streets are paved with gold, and whose valleys flow with milk and honey. In the centre of this enormous city, you are told that there is a "GREAT WHITE THRONE" of alabaster, upon which is seated GOD, with a sceptre in his hand, which he sways relentlessly over the heads of those immaculate saints who have been so lucky as to find favor in his eyes. At his right hand are seated his cabinet, who have in charge the "Book of life,"—in which are kept the records of each saint's life,—which is to be opened when the last trump shall sound, and the account between God and each soul balanced. In front of this throne is a Bar, called the bar of God, before which each soul is to be arraigned to receive its sentence. On the left hand of the throne are seated the souls of the saints, whose only employment is to sing pæans of praise to the "King of kings."

Now many may deem this account of Heaven *blasphemous*,—and indeed it is;—but nevertheless it is the account, *verbatim et literatim*, given every day in your churches, to which fact every honest man will attest. Reader, what think you? Does this idea of Heaven give you very exalted ideas either of God, or the ends of human life? Does it serve as an incentive to moral and intellectual progression? I know your answers: I shall read them from your soul, as you scan these pages.

Let us see: Heaven, they tell you, is "New Jerusalem," with pavements of gold. Now ask yourself what possible pleasure *God*, the author of all things, could find in *material* splendor? If this idea of Heaven be correct, then Heaven is a *material* world, and will be occupied by *material* beings,—flesh and blood. This *too* is claimed by your priests; for they tell you that, "there is to be a grand day of Judgment,—a day when the dead, both small and great, shall be called before God, to be judged;" when the dust of their bodies is to be gathered from the four quarters of the Earth, and again placed "*in form;*" when the same blood that *now* flows through your veins will be quickened into circulation, and yourselves become, after long ages of death-slumber, "*yourselves* again."

The absurdity of notions of this kind will appear evident to you from the following truths, — truths that are advanced and conceded by a large portion of the orthodox world. God is an immutable being; He is the author of all things. He established the laws which govern all things; and those laws, like himself, are immutable. He never has changed, nor will change them, because they are *perfect*, and need no change. These propositions are advanced by the most orthodox portion of the world, and are known to be truths by all sensible beings. Then it follows, the laws of nature being immutable, that the relation between flesh and spirit can never be changed, but must ever remain the same.

Now the natural tendency of flesh is gross, — of spirit, refined; unite flesh and spirit, and, as a natural and inevitable result, grossness will follow. Hence, if man's ultimate spiritual progression is to be crowned with a *material* body, it follows, as a natural consequence, that he will again become a being possessed of *gross* propensities, and have to *re*-fight the battle attendant upon a union of flesh and spirit. Hence Heaven, instead of being the abode of immaculate saints, will be as much a theatre of sin, folly, turmoil and strife, as the Earth is now. — What object can there be in paving the streets of Heaven with gold, unless it be to gratify the miserly feelings of those who enter in at the gates of the "New

Jerusalem"? Of what use can the rivers of milk and honey be, unless to feed the greedy appetites of those who abide upon their banks?

Let me ask you candidly, — do you believe that God is so fond of flattery, as to create men simply to be his flatterers? You answer, *No*. Then let me ask you, — can you accredit the common notions of the day in reference to him and Heaven? Most certainly not; for if you do, then you must believe God to be a *vain* being, and Heaven the theatre of his vanity; for you are told that the *sole* occupation of saints is to sing pæans of praise to God. Does this contemplate a very high state of life for man? It converts heaven into a grand camp-meeting, where, from age to age, shouts and songs will unceasingly ring, and fall sweetly on the ear of him, who created man after his own image, and pronounced him good.

These ideas are false, and your *own* reason rejects them. Man was not created simply to be a puppet, but is a progressive being, as I have before said, and will reap happiness proportioned to his spiritual condition when he throws off his mortal coil, and becomes a *spiritual* being. Base not your ideas of the soul's future condition upon empty nonsense, but learn from nature the important truth; let reason teach you, and all will be well. God keeps no books of debt and credit, balances no accounts; — your own soul is the parchment, whereon are written your virtues and your vices. Be careful that the former predominate, and in the spirit land you will reap happiness and joy. Put the talents, given you by nature, into the hands of the usurer, — unfold, cultivate, develop the powers of the soul, and you will meet the requirements of Nature and Nature's God.

I have said that the ultimate of matter is not met in man, but that he has within himself a principle of intelligence or spirit, that *commences* its development in the body, and continues it in celestial regions;—hence man must physically die. Notwithstanding the perfect confidence which many tell you they feel in the existence and power of God, but a few of the thousands, who are daily ushered into eternity, approach their death-beds without feelings of fear and horror. They look forward into the vista of the future, and fear that, perchance, they *may* be mistaken in reference to their immortality, and hence cling to *life* with the utmost tenacity. Doubts lurk in their minds, and they cannot go to the grave

"Like him who wraps the drapery of his couch about him,
And lies down to pleasant dreams,"—

but fearfully, reluctantly approach it, as the grand *finale* of all life and pleasure. By all classes, Christians, Infidels, &c., Death is looked upon as a huge monster, going about seeking whom it may devour; and when at last they feel its presence, they fain would arrest its power, and ward off the fatal hour. But the human hand cannot stay it. When the arrow is set in the bow, it surely strikes its mark, and high and low, Christian and Infidel, alike fall victims.

This fear of death arises from the doubts that people entertain in reference to God, and the immortality of the soul. To alleviate the dread of this phase of life, spirits came from their happy homes to show their earthly friends that there is in store for *all* an immortal existence; but men in their boastfulness reject them, and say they never had a doubt as to their immortality. And yet it is a fact that but few have perfect faith in an immortal existence. Faith is not knowledge. People, who will take the trouble, can learn from us the *fact* of immortality, and hence have every doubt removed. How many a one, since we first began to make our demonstrations, who has refused to receive our visits, when laid low upon the bed of death, have wished that they *had* examined our claims! They find that they need more than faith to sustain them in that trying hour,—they wish for knowledge. And how many there now are, who are rejecting us and our advocates, who, under the same circumstances, will repent in "sack-cloth and ashes" that they did not investigate the matter!

I have passed the valley of the *shadow* of death, and it may be pleasing to many to learn something in relation to that point in life which is so *generally* dreaded. When the physical energies become attenuated by age, or disease, the soul struggles to cast off its fetters, and death ensues. Under different circumstances, the *pangs* of death differ; but upon physical dissolution, commonly, there is but slight pain,—the most severe pain precedes the falling off of the pulse. When the blood ceases to act forcibly, the heart lessens its beats, and so weak becomes the state of the system, that the lamp of life goes out as sweetly as one would, after severe exhaustion, fall in the arms of refreshing sleep. The pain, when one dies from disease of an exhausting character, is seldom severe; but when one is stricken down by an accidental hand, in the full vigor of life, health and strength, the pain is very severe. The spirit commences its departure from the body as soon as the heart ceases its beatings, and the blood its ebb and flow.

Usually as soon as the damp of dissolution seats itself upon the system, the spirit is given the power of perceiving its guardians, who are continually hovering about it, to cheer its entrance into the Spirit Land. This perception of guardians with me, and in fact with nearly all who have died, was given some few moments after my physical powers had been dampened forever. A brilliantly intense light shoots in upon the soul,—it sees flitting about it ethereal beings, familiar in countenance, &c., and hears confused voices, whisperings and angelic music, such as the human ear has not yet been blessed with. It becomes confused and overwhelmed by the scene, and deems the whole a dream; but in a short space of time the joyful reality bursts upon its vision. Angel friends flock around it to greet its arrival to its new home, and the happy spirit confidently and joyfully embraces old friends and kindred, and thanks God that it is free from the miserable existence of Earth. It finds itself in possession of new powers. In *stead* of perceiving things through the gross organs of the body, it finds itself *intuitively* perceiving them. Instead of desiring to *re*-enjoy the pleasures of Earth, it loathes them, and wonders that it could ever have enjoyed its delights. It is conducted through the blissful regions by its guardians and friends, and, by *affinity*, is left to choose its circle of associates and friends. When located, the spirit commences the work of progression.

I wish in this place to correct a few erroneous impressions that have been commonly entertained, and frequently honestly entertained, in reference to my own death. When I was upon Earth, I was well known to the orthodox world as *Thomas Paine*, or, in common parlance, as "*Tom Paine;*" and by my various writings upon theological subjects, that were considerable obstacles in their way, gained the entire disapprobation of the *soi-disant* Christians. When on Earth my name was associated with everything evil, and used as a sort of accompaniment with the word devil. Children, by their pious parents, were taught to regard me as a sort of "devil incarnate," and, at the mention of my name, would hug closely to their mother's knees, and, reposing their little heads upon her lap, would hardly dare breathe, lest Tom Paine and the devil should happen along, and take them to infernal regions. This superstitious fear impregnated the minds of these children with such holy horror of me, that time cannot eradicate it; and hence, at this day, the most foul and scandalous opprobriums that the human mind can conceive are heaped upon my memory, and my grave is regarded by many as the gateway to hell.

Unable to attack successfully my *writings*, honest (?) priests and laymen have attacked, and still do attack me personally. Various works are extant, concocted by foul-mouthed villains, entitled, "Life of Thomas Paine," which are as destitute of truth as they might be expected to be, coming from the *authors* that claim the honor of their penning. As to the incorrectness of these books, I will point out but one falsehood,—and that is in relation to my death. It is claimed, and believe by the religious world, that I died a most *excruciating* and *horrible* death; that my screams for mercy, and prayers of repentance, were so loud as to deafen all other sounds within a "quarter of a mile of the 'hovel' in which I died." It is said I desired a priest to be called *in*, that I might be prayed for, and find favor in the sight of God; that I denounced my writings, &c., &c., to infinity.

I now take occasion to pronounce these assertions and records as *wilfully* and *maliciously false.* I died *quietly* and *calmly*, with little pain, and no terror. I felt supported and sustained in my dying hour by a consciousness that my life had not been in vain, and that I had lived and acted as an *honest* man should. I was too *independent*, too reckless of the favor of the world, to purchase it by being a hypocrite. What I believed, I would speak, and no mortal could prevent it. I believed the world to be in error, as I still do. I *fought* those errors, and I still intend to fight them, and may be able to throw some truths before the world, that will give an impetus to religious inquiry.

Be not afraid of death,—it is but a pleasant transit from things of earth to a blissful life in celestial regions, a throwing off of the mortal coil, in which the soul is chained, to take up a higher and better life. Let the chief efforts of your earthly life be to attain intellectual and moral worth, and death will bring no terrors, the grave gain no victory.

CHAPTER VI.

SPIRIT.

I HAVE said that man is possessed of an *immortal* principle,—or principle of intelligence,—called Spirit, and it behoves us in this place to speak more fully than we have done *of* this principle. It is impossible for me to describe the composition of the Soul. I will simply say that Spirit is a *substance*, but so sublimated, so refined, as to be intangible, imperceptible to the *human* senses. It is the essential and life-giving power of *all* things. Without this spiritual principle, nothing can exist; yet it varies in its conditions, refinement, &c., as it has become progressed and developed. All "matter contains within itself, in embryo, undeveloped life" to infinity, which by various processes is brought forth from its latent condition, and developed. Vegetables of all classes, as well as animals, possess this principle in a greater or less degree.

We have before seen that man is the highest ultimate of matter, and that he came up, by regular stages of gradation, from the lowest point of animal life, to his present perfect form;—hence it follows, that *man* is more *purely* a spiritual being than any other of the animal kingdom. In him the spirit is more fully developed, and hence he is not simply a being of *instinctive* powers, but possesses the powers of reason, that are the highest qualities of spirit, and which enable it to unfold, develop itself, and perform the grand mission for which it was designed.

In this place it may be well for me to say, that notwithstanding vegetables, and animals below man, possess a spiritual principle, they do not exist in the Spirit Land as spiritual beings. It has often been asked of spirits, whether animals exist here in *spirit*, and the answer has been *yes.* This error has arisen from this fact; animals do not in *reality* exist here, — but in one way they do, — they exist in *representation.* Whatever a Spirit *desires* to perceive, is at once perceived, either being mirrored from its own memory, or from the memory of those about it. I may here state that the Spirit Land is a perfect representation of each of its societies. There are here *seven* circles or spheres of life, which are yet divided into other minor circles or grades, to a great number.

I have before said, and will now *re*-say, that the inceptive condition of a Spirit in this land is just as its condition was when on Earth. Hence, if a person is possessed of gross propensities, and has neglected the development of the moral and intellectual powers of the Spirit when on Earth, upon its arrival here, it is placed in the first or second circle of existence, just as it is *extremely* or partially gross. If one has developed the powers of the Spirit, and paid due attention to its unfolding, it is placed in the third, fourth, or fifth circle, just in proportion to its *progressed* state *morally* and intellectually. I say *placed* in these circles, — perhaps it will be well to explain. Spirits are free to choose their circle or society when they enter this region; but it is invariably the case, that, in its selection, it is governed by its affinity. As spirits in the body seek *congenial* spirits for associates and companions, so they do here; and thus here you may find low and undeveloped spirits seeking *equally* low and undeveloped spirits, in order that they may find companions in their shame, and a degree of consolation in their misery, from a knowledge that they are not *alone* in their degradation. The power of affinity is stronger here than on Earth, because each spirit at once perceives *its* condition, as well as the condition of those about it, and cannot endure the presence and society of those who are more perfectly developed.

In each of these different circles and societies the Spirit Land appears differently. It is a perfect image of each society, and does not appear in all its beauty until perfect development of the powers of the spirit. Each spirit enjoys its particular delight in *idea*, and not in reality; though these imaginings are regarded by many *as*, and supposed to be *real*. Hence, when the question in reference to the existence of animals in this land is asked, some spirits tell you that they *do* abide here, — others that they do not; and both answer you, as they believe, truthfully.

The Spirit of man attains its form and stature in the body, — and his spiritual body or form is a perfect type of the physical; hence you will be able to discern your friends and acquaintances here readily and easily.

When the infant dies, its little spirit is transported hither, and ushered into the presence of its friends, who attend upon it with affectionate care, and aid and assist in the development of its intellectual and moral powers, — though in stature, form and size, it will ever be an infant. This infantile spiritual condition arises from this fact, that at birth one has not the same amount of spiritual essence as at middle or mature age; for, as the physical powers are enlarged, developed by age, culture, food, &c., so are the spiritual; as the physical powers extract nourishment and *increase* from food, so do the spiritual. This to many may seem strange; — but remember that all matter has its due proportion of spiritual essence, which essentially exists, and increases the size, power and vigor of both the spirit of higher and lower orders of animals. The spiritual part of food is taken up by the spirit of the one using it, and forms part and parcel of that immortal power that survives physical dissolution, and falls not beneath the dire strokes of Time. Infants, though ever infants in stature, may yet progress intellectually; they may unfold, develop the powers given them, but can never attain remarkable intellectual power.

As the infant in form, stature, features, &c., ever remains an infant, so does every other Spirit assume and hold forever, form, features, stature, &c., which are a perfect type of the physical body

The tendency of Spirit, as I have before said, like all matter, is progressive. The Spirit, upon assuming an independent existence, will, *must* progress, — it will not, cannot retrograde. The powers of the Spirit, in its independent state, are numerous and extensive. It has none of the physical wants of the body to supply; its wants and powers are purely spiritual. It does not see, hear, speak, smell, &c., as does the Spirit in the body, but knows all things by intuition. Its powers of locomotion are rapid, and its perception almost limitless. It is not a fact that a Spirit can fly with the rapidity of thought from point to point, though it can, and does perform aërial journeys with great haste. If a Spirit be interrogated here, with reference to the condition of certain matters in France, it is not always absolutely necessary that it should pass thither to answer you, for its powers of discernment are so wonderful, as to bring a perception of the matter to itself at once, — though not always is this the case. Spirits do not perceive *material* things, but simply their spiritual part. Spirits are more sublimated and ethereal in their composition than even electricity, and hence pass through physical substances with ease. Not being *able* to perceive *material* things, these do not obstruct its passage.

Spirits being, upon their entrance here, both *morally* and intellectually as they were at physical death, necessarily differ upon theological and other subjects; but the higher and more progressed spirits agree. The occupations of Spirits are such as are compatible with their tastes. Those inclined to intellectual pursuits continue them with great avidity and facility; for the perceptive powers of Spirits are so strong, their powers of locomotion so great, that hardly anything is hidden from them. Those inclined to scientific investigations, continue them here, and so each one follows the bent of his inclinations.

Notwithstanding the faculties possessed by us, we are not infinite in power. We are not Gods, but Spirits — progressive beings — learning new truths each hour of our existence, and perfecting ourselves as rapidly as possible. Persons have many erroneous impressions in relation to our powers, and propound to us questions that none but God could answer. It is generally supposed that Spirits must be perfect — that they can never err — and that all Spirits are *alike* in knowledge and power. This is wrong. The future is hidden from *us*, as well as yourselves, hence it is not possible for us to impart to you any information in reference thereto, save only as we judge from *present* circumstances. If it were otherwise even, it would not be proper for us to unfold to you its secrets, for wisely has man been denied the power of knowing that which *is* to be in his earthly career: — did he know, life would lose its zest. The vail of the future by mortal or spiritual eyes cannot be penetrated, and the millions of events that are in *embryo* in its bosom must be waited for — they cannot be known until foreshadowed or developed.

CHAPTER VII.

SPIRIT LAND.

Each of the inhabited planets has its Spirit Land, or place of repose for the soul, when it passes from the physical fetters with which it is bound whilst in the body. This Land, as we have called it, is situated above the atmosphere, and is a perfect type, *generally*, of the planet to which it belongs — though beautified. The Spirit Land, like Spirit itself, is purely ethereal, and a shadow of the memory and imagination of each Spirit. The Spirits of each planet, when advanced to the Sixth circle, can commune and visit with each other.

I have before said that the Spirit Land appears differently to its different societies, and is only seen in all its beauty when the faculties of the soul have become developed. The desire of each Spirit is gratified *seemingly*, though not really. Hence the miser, whose *sole* delight on Earth was to hoard up and count his dollars, in the first circle is gratified with imaginary dollars, which he hoards up, clutches, chuckles over, counts, with as much delight and avariciousness as when on Earth. In *idea* he is gratified, and this *idea seems* reality, yet is not. Misers congregate in separate societies from affinity. The predominating desire governs in the selection of societies, though not so in relation to circles. It would be a pleasing spectacle to you to behold millions of avaricious souls congregated together, eagerly bent on counting over and stowing away their imaginary treasures; to see the suspicious glances cast upon each other, the *fear* depicted in their countenances, the tiptoe tread, as they go to and from the haunt of, or hiding-place for their treasures; — in a word, to see the prominent traits of their character and disposition mirrored forth from their souls, and acted by them. But to *us* who have progressed, it is *not* a pleasing sight, and we use our utmost efforts to root out and destroy these desires — which we are able in time to do — and instigate the possessors to moral and intellectual progression.

The miser has his Heaven, and were you to ask him in relation to the Spirit Land, he would tell you that he was enjoying himself finely — making money, &c. His appreciation of Heaven does not transcend the *dollar*. But this is only the case in their inceptive condition here, for their attention is soon turned otherwise, and they come to *lose* their pleasures, and seek for higher and better occupations.

A person of a poetical temperament and *ideal* mind has his Heaven, which is a perfect daguerreotype of his imagination. Interrogate him in relation thereto, and he will tell you that he is surrounded by gentle hills, extensive plains, majestic mountains, swelling seas, running rivers, gurgling brooks, sparkling fountains, leaping rills, foaming cataracts, wide-spread forests—all echoing and reëchoing with the songs of birds, and peopled to a limitless extent with creatures of fancy. To *him* this is a reality, and yet it is *not* a reality.

The sailor, whose chief delight on Earth was to stem the fury of the sea, embarks in his imaginary ship, with comrades of the same desire, upon an imaginary sea—unfurls the sails, feels the imaginary winds, hears their whistle in the rigging, and sees and feels all the attending circumstances of a voyage upon the "deep." The face of the sky is eagerly watched, each portending circumstance prepared for. Clouds arise in the horizon—storms burst in fury upon the sea, the waves roll and dash, the lightnings flash and play along the sky, the deep thunder rolls upon his ear, and he feels all those emotions attendant upon the *reality*.

The Indian, whose delights were in the forest chase, and war, *enjoys* here his delights, and in his imaginary world feels and acts as under a reality. Thus you will perceive that the Spirit Land bears different phases, proportioned to each one's desires, and is a general type of the Earth, or its peculiar planet. These desires, in time, are satiated, and progression ensues.

To give you a correct idea of the Spirit Land, it will

be necessary for me to say that it is divided into circles, or tribes, as we will term them, each of which is possessed of peculiar characteristics, and from the first, upwards, is a step in the ladder of spiritual progression. Of this Land there are seven *grand* divisions, each of which, except the seventh, is yet divided into other *societies* to a great number. The first circle is the circle or tribe with which are connected all Spirits of the most *gross* propensities, and who have been guilty of the lowest species of crime which is possible to be perpetrated on Earth.

I have before said that the Spirit of man is the grand parchment whereon are written his virtues and his vices, and I may here say, that here, in this spiritual home, this record stands forth in bold relief, and each good and bad deed that one has committed is not screened — but read by all. The hypocrite, who on Earth has masked his vices and *seemed* a saint, is here unable to conceal them: — they stand forth in legible and intelligible characters, and it is the consciousness of this that attracts Spirits to those of their kind, as I have before said.

The First Circle is the lowest and most inharmonious circle of spiritual existence. It is the theatre of inharmony, such as you might imagine to exist on Earth, should there be congregated in a mass all the vicious elements of society; for it is the retreat of those who have neglected the development of those faculties of the soul whose development *alone* elevates man above the brutes. The murderer, the pirate, highwayman, thief, hypocrite, liar, libertine, drunkard, incendiary, slanderer, miser, &c., &c., is there — of all nations and tongues, congregated in ungainly societies, and pursuing their various occupations with a double vigor, pushed on by the pangs of conscience, that lead them to hide their vices by still deeper indulgence in them.

I have before said that this circle is divided into societies, and that, in the formation and selection of these societies, the predominating desire governs; hence those, who on Earth have delighted in the shedding of human blood, assemble *en masse*, and pursue their murderous career with vigor. They use imaginary weapons, and commit imaginary murders. They are continually in turmoil and strife. Like the Ishmaelite, each one's hand is turned against the other's. Imagine to yourself, on Earth, two persons of gross propensities engaged in a quarrel; imagine the quarrel to have attained that point when a dagger is drawn by one of the parties. Behold the person upon whom it is drawn fleeing from his murderous foe, who, with drawn dagger, tightly clenched, is on the chase, uttering unearthly curses and cries for vengeance. Imagine the pursuer to near the pursued, raise his dagger, and with a single stroke draw his heart's blood. See the guilty man, when the awful deed is done, stricken with fear and remorse, eagerly seeking to screen the body from the public eye, and blot out all traces of the deed — and you have in *miniature* the condition of *this* society of the first circle. Millions of souls, upon whom are deep stains of blood, in one congregated brotherhood of crime, are there engaged in a series of turmoil and inhuman deeds.

In the same circle, and in an equally low society, may be seen the pirate — who embarks on the voyage of murderous theft, and commits depredations upon his "fellow-voyagers on the deep," akin to those it was his delight to commit when on Earth. The same phases of life that attended him on Earth attend him here. His imaginary cannon bellow forth their thunder, and send forth their murderous balls, carrying destruction and desolation to the imaginary craft that his vengeance is being wreaked upon. The vessels are thrown alongside, and, hand to hand, with desperate fury, he fights for his prize;— many a victim *seems* to fall beneath his strokes, and with a yell of satisfaction, and maniac brutality, he surveys the bloody deck, and clutches his dearly-bought treasures. To him all seems a reality; but he has fought but empty air, and gained an unreal prize.

The highwayman, who on earth delighted in deeds of daring and robbery, here follows his favorite pursuits, and *re*-enjoys all the pleasures attendant upon such a life on earth. In this society are *all* thieves. The debauchee is there, and, in a bacchanalian society, imaginarily satisfies his appetites, and feels all those exhilarating thrills — and relapses — that were his lot on earth. This society is the most beastly in this circle, for in it are committed all species of crime, and are exhibited all conditions of debasement. The bacchanalian song echoes and *re*-echoes through their ranks, until the vault of *this* part of Heaven rings with one unceasing, discordant shout. Libertines and harlots are there, and, burning with remorse, would fain enjoy the delights of passion. Oh! it is an awful spectacle, to behold human souls writhing in the agonies that do this society of the first circle! — but we are cheered by the glorious thought that reformatory influences will operate upon its members, and in time relieve their degradation and misery. The discordant elements of which this circle is composed at times mingle, and Oh! it is sad to see the debasement of which the human soul is susceptible, as it is portrayed in these minglings; and, were you to see the misery that is there, you would think that it was Hell enough for any one.

This circle is only occupied by those of the *lowest* development, and there, through long ages of mental torment, are congregated miserable and unhappy souls, who, in time, will change their lives, in accordance with the unceasing and effectual law of progression, and pass to higher circles. Good Spirits, actuated by philanthropic and elevated motives, are continually laboring with, to reform and elevate them; and it is a joyful victory for us when we induce one soul after another to yield to moral influences, cast aside its miserable fetters, that have bound it to crime, and *progress*. It should be the aim of every man on Earth to so live as to avoid this circle; for its miseries are such as cannot be described, but only known when felt and seen.

This idea of the First Circle of the Spirit Land may to some seem strange — but nevertheless, it is *its true* condition; and of this you will be satisfied when you remember that man is a *progressive* being, and can only attain a high state of existence as he develops and unfolds his spiritual principle.

The Second Circle is composed of Spirits who are more advanced than those of the First Circle, though, in this circle even, there is not to be found that moral and intellectual state of development that one would expect. This is the abiding place of those whose lives were not particularly vicious, but who are in an undeveloped condition, — those who have neglected their spiritual development for physical pleasure and profit. In a word, it is the home of ignorant Spirits. There are also to be found in this circle the Spirits of many who have progressed thither from the First Circle. In this circle are by far the greatest number of Spirits: for it is a fact that the number of ignorant Spirits, launched into eternity annually, exceeds the number of developed Spirits in a ratio of about 1000 to 1.

In this circle are the people of all nations and tongues. The Aborigines and various other people who have remained in an unprogressed intellectual and moral state.

This circle is divided into societies. In one group may be seen mechanics engaged in their favorite occupations; in another, the farmer, who is tilling his imaginary farm, and engaged in agricultural pursuits generally. And thus, all through this circle, may be found societies made up by affinity of desires, — each one pursuing his or her favorite occupation. This circle is surrounded with a more moral atmosphere than the first, and exhibits a more progressed condition. Progression is more rapidly secured by its inmates, as good spirits find less difficulty in approaching it.

The Second Circle is much more harmonious than the First, though, from the ignorance of its inmates, perfect harmony could by no possibility exist. Over this circle, missionary Spirits, from the Fifth and Sixth Circles, have strong care, and labor assiduously to unfold the powers of the inmates. The attention of each, by these missionaries, is gradually turned toward intellectual and moral pursuits, and in course of time they become progressed so far as to exchange their residence for the Third Circle, which is the abiding place of Spirits who are more highly developed than those of the Second.

The Third Circle is occupied by Spirits well-meaning and disposed, but who have neglected to unfold the intellectual powers of the soul,—who have no, or, at most, but a partial acquaintance with Nature and her laws, so that they are unfitted to live in harmony therewith. In this circle there is a moral beauty displayed, that is seen in none of the lower circles, and which places it far, very far in advance of them. Therein are many Spirits of considerable literary talents, and scientific research, who abide in groups, according to their affinities of taste.

The occupation of the members of this circle is purely progressive; they are engaged in developing and unfolding their powers by discipline and research. To this circle are the Spirits of infants and undeveloped children consigned, who are watched over, attended and educated with the utmost care and attention. The principle of love is more fully developed in this circle than any other, and its inmates exhibit remarkable benevolence and kindness in their demeanor, one towards another. After a sufficient study of Nature, and an attainment of the requisite wisdom, the inmates of this circle progress to the Fourth Circle, where the beauties of the Spirit Land begin to appear with force and perspicuity;—for this circle, besides being surrounded with an exceedingly *moral* atmosphere, is occupied by wise Spirits, as Love and Wisdom are the prevailing principles in development. Spirits of this circle are highly progressed,—it being the abiding place of *many* scientific, literary and educated persons. This circle is also divided into societies, made up as the preceding are.

The grand effort and aim of the Spirits of this circle is to attain *Truth*, which, owing to their superior wisdom and moral condition, they are able to do with much greater facility than are the members of the Third. The less progressed are assisted by those more developed, and thus, each mutually assisting the other, they are all hastening to the point when they can be admitted into the Fifth Circle, which is the highest circle possible to be reached by the new-born Spirit from the body.

This circle is composed of Spirits who have strenuously labored while on Earth to develop and unfold the *full* powers of the soul, and by those who have come up thither from the lower circles. Herein are exhibited the powers of the Spirit when unfolded by the discipline of thought and research. Love, Wisdom and Truth beam forth from the countenances of each, and a degree of power and harmony exists, that the human mind is not able to appreciate. The number of societies is less than in any lower circle, and there is a more general exchange of thought and sympathy than is possible to exist in any of the lower circles, or on Earth.

This circle is composed of moral and wise Spirits, whose chief study is Nature, and whose chief aim is to secure harmony and fraternal union. Intellectual and moral pursuits are prosecuted with vigor and success. Various sciences are studied and perfected, with a view to unfold the spiritual powers, and prepare for that grand Harmonial State, between which and their own circle there is but an intermediate step.

The members of this circle make many visits to

Earth, and glean all the truths possible from the minds of the most eminent scholars thereon. But in this way but little knowledge, comparatively, is gained; — from their powers of perception, they find more advantage in a study of Nature. It requires but a short space of time, comparatively, with assiduous attention and application, to prepare for and be ushered into the Sixth Circle, which is the seat of a moral beauty, intellectual grandeur and harmony, that the human faculties cannot conceive or comprehend. Almost perfect harmony exists throughout this circle, and Love, Wisdom and Truth seem to be stamped upon all. There is a mingling of thought and sympathy, between the societies of this circle, that is not to be found in the lower circles; there is a sort of mutual affinity and desire to assist each other in progressive advancement, that is ultimately to be consummated in the Seventh Circle.

Between the members of this circle and the inhabitants of the Spirit Land of Jupiter, and all the planets that have attained the same point of progression, there are mutual exchanges of thoughts, and visits, that are enjoyed by none of the occupants of the lower circles. These visits and exchanges are frequent, profitable and necessary, as they serve to prepare each other for that point when the Spirits of all planets are to be united in one grand circle of harmonious union.

The number of Spirits in the Sixth Circle is much less than in any other circle. This is a kind of probationary state for the Spirit. Its chief designs and efforts are to attain a *perfect* knowledge of *all* truth, within the scope of its conditional powers, — for, without this desire, there would, nor can be harmony of opinion and action. The faculties possessed by the members of this circle to attain knowledge and truth are extensive, and comparatively unlimited; and these faculties are employed to great advantage. All the noblest attributes of the soul are developed, and when finally developed, the possessor can pass from this circle to the Third Sphere, or Seventh Circle.

The Seventh Circle is not connected solely with the Spirit Land of our particular planet, but is, as it were, a new world, wherein are congregated the harmonized souls of *all* planets and nations. The beauty of this circle I cannot tell you from experience, as it has not yet been my privilege to visit it. The inhabitants of that sphere never pay *you* visits, nor ourselves, but commune with us by influx; and thus have I gained a partial knowledge of the blissful retreat, whither the fully progressed soul ultimately goes.

Thousands of years are spent by us in fitting ourselves for that sphere,—and the process, by which we pass thither, is almost equivalent to another dissolution. There are in the Sixth Circle Spirits who have been here engaged in the grand work of development for many centuries, and who have not yet sufficiently unfolded the harmonial powers of the soul, to be fitted for that sphere where all is harmony and peace,—where the beauty of the Divine mind is seen in *all* its splendor, and the soul of man transformed into an *almost* perfect existence.

This circle, as it is commonly denominated, is more properly a *Sphere*. It has no connection with the individual Heavens, but is a grand Sphere, where are united all developed Spirits of *all* worlds.

The occupations of the Spirits in this sphere are such as are compatible with their natural desires, in the pursuit of which each mutually assists the other. Therein is to be found a combination of Love, Wisdom and

Truth, such as is beyond the powers of your minds to conceive.

In speaking of the Seventh Circle, I have said that it is the home of those Spirits who have attained *perfect* development,— which if, in the common signification of the word, was the case, the progression of the soul is consummated, and would cease; — but I have used the words *perfect* and *fully*, *comparatively:* I would have them signify such a state of progression as to your minds would appear *perfect*, but which, nevertheless, is *not* perfect; but such a state of moral and mental progression, that the *human mind* could conceive no further progression possible. Spirits are progressive, and their progression is *infinite*, unceasing, eternal; their object is to attain *perfect* development, yet perfection cannot be attained by them. They aim at an attainment of the knowledge of *all* truth, but nevertheless can *never* attain this knowledge; for should they do so, or were they able to do so, they would cease to be *finite*, and would become *infinite* beings, — and hence Deities in knowledge and power.

The Seventh Circle, or Third Sphere, is a grand *Harmonial* Sphere, and, unlike the lower state of Spirits, is not divided into societies, but is one *grand* society, the efforts of whose members are to develop their own, and mutually assist each other in the development of spiritual powers. There is about this sphere a moral and intellectual beauty that is dazzling to behold, and impossible to describe or conceive, until seen and known.

I have said, in a preceding page, that the tendency of Spirit is progressive, and that it cannot by any possibility retrograde. By this I mean that *eternal* retrogression is impossible; but that, although in its inceptive stages of existence it may (in the First Circle) retrograde, this retrocession *will*, and *must* end in progression. I will here take occasion to say that, save in the First Circle, there is no *retrogression*,— but *progression* stamps the efforts, and is the motto of all Spirits.

The account which I have given of the Spirit Land differs, in very many of its points, very materially from the accounts given you by various spiritual clairvoyants, — as Swedenborg, Davis, the clairvoyants employed by Cahagnet, &c., — which conflicts will appear to you as necessary consequences of propositions before laid down by me; that the Spirit Land is a perfect type of each spirit's desires and powers, and is only seen in its *true* state when the spirit has attained sufficient progression to enter the Sixth Circle of existence. That the various circles are made up by affinity of desires, and that, by no possibility, can the Spirit in the body go beyond the Fifth Circle of development.

Now you will at once perceive that a clairvoyant, being in a spiritual ecstacy, would naturally gravitate to that circle for which he had an affinity, and would perceive such a spiritual state as was compatible with his own prejudices, powers, &c. Hence Swedenborg, being educated *to*, and prejudiced in favor *of*, a belief in the "Holy Writ" (so called), would perceive in the Spirit Land such a state or condition of life as was compatible *with* those prejudices, because his prejudices would exist in *representation* before him. Hence *he*, believing in the existence of "hell torments for the wicked, in a lake that burneth with fire and brimstone," tells you that he saw *in* the Spirit Land not solely *a* Hell, but Hells, burning as aforesaid, compatible with his views.

No two *Spiritual* Clairvoyants have ever yet given you like accounts of the spiritual condition; and yet this difference of accounts does not militate against the *genuineness* of their powers, but simply illustrates the truth of what I have said in relation to the Spirit Land being a perfect type of each spirit's desires, powers, &c., — these desires and prejudices being before them in "REPRESENTATION." Davis was less prejudiced than Swedenborg, as his mind had not been subjected to the discipline of the strait-jacket of sectarianism, or a great degree of *any* species of education, — hence his powers were in a more *natural* or favorable condition to perceive, more nearly than Swedenborg, the spiritual state. Yet, if you compare the account of the Spirit Land, given by him, with his phrenological developments, and state of education at the time, you will find that it is such an account as would naturally be expected from him, in accordance with the statement before made, that "each Spirit perceives such a condition as is compatible with his desires, powers, education," &c. Mr. Davis, as nearly as was possible for him, gave what he saw in the spiritual plane, but yet did not give you a correct account. Not, however, were these errors the result of any wilful or *intentional* purpose to inculcate error, but for the reasons before stated; — and here allow me to say, that, as a *man*, Mr. Davis has not his equal on your globe. He is actuated by the most *pure* intentions, and is a highly advanced Spirit. His motives are *purely* philanthropic, and there does not exist within him, in development, a vicious principle. Yet Mr. D.'s account of the Spirit Land you will perceive to be widely different from Swedenborg's.

Mr. Cahagnet, of France, through clairvoyants employed by him, has issued to the world opinions in reference to this sphere, which widely differ from either of the preceding, and from the same cause. The clairvoyants employed by him were but slightly susceptible of spiritual ecstasies, and withal were in an imperfect state of development in *every* respect, and not very well calculated to give the world much light upon either spiritual or human matters. By these clairvoyants many exceedingly imperfect accounts were given, and such as are, in fact, in conflict with themselves.

The idea is there advanced that the apparel of each Spirit, in the body, is impregnated with spiritual emanations that enable it to exist here; hence that each Spirit is able to appear in any of its "bodily" apparel that it pleases, or in such apparel as it wore on Earth. Now this, in one respect, is incorrect. The clothes of an individual are not able to obtain an existence here, from any spiritual emanations with which they become impregnated; but Spirits may *appear* to be dressed in their peculiar earthly apparel, if *they* desire so to do, or if other Spirits desire them so to do, — but not because their clothes *spiritually* exist, though they do exist in *representation*, or are mirrored from the memory, at the desire of the Spirit.

I have given you but a general account of the spiritual condition. It would be impossible for me to enter into minute details in one or twenty volumes; but, from the facts given, you will draw as perfect an idea thereof, as you would from a more minute account. The account given is correct, and may be relied on. It has passed through no *human* brain, nor been subjected to any human influences. The medium, through whom I write, is purely for me *mechanical*, and can, by *no possibility*, influence the language or ideas of the volume. From my observation and study, together with actual experience, I write, and what I have written is correct *in toto.*.

Spirits retain their affections for their kindred and earthly friends, and pay them many visits to learn their condition. They exercise over them a watchful care, and ofttimes *influence* their minds, — and in more ways than one have an influence on their lives and fortunes. You are indebted to them for very many suggestions and thoughts, that come to you, you know not how. Mothers, with a purer and holier affection than mortals possess, hover near and watch their children in the body, ofttimes preserving them from error and danger by operating upon their minds. Could you see the angel friends that are often hovering about you, at day and even-time, with noiseless tread, watching your daily avocations and your slumbers, your hearts would rejoice to think that Heaven and Earth were so near together.

Each Spirit *in* the body has his or her guardian or guardians, who are oftentimes near them, influencing their actions, and breathing quiet and hope into their minds. These guardians choose the person over whom to keep sentry, by their affinity. They choose a *congenial* spirit, sometimes of kindred, sometimes not. Spirits are drawn to, or repelled from individuals on the Earth, just as they have affinities or dislikes for those persons. Guardians are always from that circle, to which the individual, over whom they have superintendence, would go at death.

Friends meet and recognize each other here, and are much more happy in each other's presence and embraces than when on Earth. It is really pleasant to behold mothers meeting their children, from whom they have been separated by long years, and again folding them to their bosoms with maternal regard; to see brothers meeting sisters and brothers; husbands meeting wives, &c., &c., with a consciousness that they are no more to be severed by the hand of Death.

Spirits have their companions here. There is here no marrying or giving in marriage by mere legal forms, or words of mouth; but each male Spirit chooses a companion from the female Spirits, who is congenial; or rather, upon the entrance of a Spirit of either sex into the Spirit World, if the Spirit's spiritual wife or husband is there, by the laws of affinity they come together, and recognize each other as eternal partners. There are here very many Spirits whose partners or companions are still in the flesh, and who are awaiting their arrival here for the consummation of that natural and inseparable union, spiritual marriage. There are comparatively few marriages consummated on Earth that are eternal. Very few are made up from affinity of desires, tastes, &c., but in accordance with base and sordid motives, that make the hymeneal altar a funeral pile, whereon are consumed and destroyed all peace and happiness on Earth. Every person has his or her *congenial* Spirit somewhere on the Earth, and those Spirits, though they may not come together on Earth, are sure to be united here. If more care was exercised on Earth, in reference to the marriage relations, a much more moral, as well as higher mental condition would exist.

From the extreme affection which Spirits entertain for their brethren on Earth, and the interest which they take in their welfare, they have been instigated, at various periods of the world's existence, to take advantage of the Laws of Nature, and visit and commune with them, with a view to point to them the *true* aims of life, and relieve the error in which they were involved, —

which is a moral incubus on the soul, weighing down and retarding its proper development. These visits were, at an earlier period of human life, quite frequent and effective; but as mankind lost their appreciation of the ends of life, and came to bow more devoutly at the shrine of Mammon than Morality or Spiritual development, they ceased to regard these visits, and hence they became entirely ineffectual, and for a time ceased. Still at various periods these visits have been continued, but Spirits have ever found difficulty in informing people of the objects of their visits, as well as the means to make their demonstrations effectual. Even Spirits themselves did not fully understand the principles or laws by which they could communicate; and it was not until the combined wisdom of many Spirits in the Sixth Circle succeeded in ferreting out and applying those laws, that we were able to communicate with you to advantage. But recently a channel of intercourse has been opened, that will continue to be perfected, until mankind will be obliged to know that Spirits *do* come to Earth, and that they *can* and *do* possess sufficient knowledge to instruct their friends *in* the flesh, as to the aims of life and their future condition. That period is nearing, and when at length it arrives, mankind will enjoy a new phase in life, and live and act more in reference to their spiritual development, than for the gratification of mere physical desires. Then will a new Era truly dawn upon the world, and then too will the face of the Universe wear a more harmonial aspect.

Heretofore, when Spirits have attempted to open a communication with Earth, their demonstrations have been either disregarded entirely, or mistaken for the influences of a demonish power. But in the nineteenth century the arts and sciences have attained so great extension and progression, and the mind is liberalized and enlightened to such an extent, that we may safely come to you without danger of subjecting our mediums to death at the stake or in the "mill-pond," as they would have been, and in fact were, in earlier periods of the world's existence. Superstition, the twin sister of ignorance, has nearly vanished from the mind, and the Devil ceased to be regarded as powerful as heretofore,—though, even at *this* time, there are those so closely chained to ancient superstitions and customs, as to denounce our efforts as the production of his Satanic Majesty. If they would take the trouble to reflect a moment upon the result of such ideas, they would not advance them. If they allege these demonstrations to the Devil, they must certainly give him the power of Omnipresence, for at the same moment communications are being received through our agency in all parts of the world. Now, if they make him omnipresent, he certainly is equal to God in power, because he has his attributes; and certainly, if he writes all the communications given from this source, he must be omniscient. But allow me say, that the Devil, who has so long had dominance over a large class of deluded souls, is a creature of fancy, and exists solely in the human bosom, which is the seat of the only Hell, or Hells, that will ever torment mankind.

It may be desirable that I should explain the method by which we communicate with men; therefore I will now do so.

It is a fact, that at this day has come to be generally acknowledged, that there are peculiar physical and mental constitutions, who can be subjected, while in the body, to the will and power of another of a different, yet peculiar physical and mental constitution. It is well known, too, that this influence is produced by the force of magnetic currents, thrown from the body of the operator to the body of the subject. These currents are evolved and sent off from the body of the operator to the body of the subject, by the force of the action of the mind. The operator, is obliged to strain his will to the utmost tension, or, in other words, to give a treble action to the brain, which is the grand centre of the nervous system. This nervous action generates magnetism, and this magnetism, being thus generated in superabundance, is sent off by the force of the will of the operator, passes to the body of the subject, and destroys for the time, or rather paralyzes, the will of the subject, and hence makes him subject to the will of the operator.

To explain to you the *modus operandi* of this, I need but to say that the nerves of the body are electricals, and, like glass, &c., are exciters of electricity, as well as generators of magnetism. The common action of the nerves, or rather their natural condition, simply enables them to evolve a sufficient or *natural* quantity of these elements; — but any unnatural action of the nerves, or rather, an extrà action, produces a superabundance of them. Hence the reason why people under excitement can speak with greater force, or accomplish their peculiar tasks with greater ease, than when in the *natural* or unexcited state. The nerves increase their action, and generate an extra quantity of electricity and magnetism, which pass to the brain, increase its action, and hence give the possessor *extra* mental as well as physical power.

It is well known that *all* are not subject to this mesmeric or magnetic action of mind upon mind, and that a peculiar physical state or condition must be possessed by the subject,—and the most essential quality requisite is nervousness; for the nerves of the subject must be slightly paralyzed, in order for the operator to gain control over the subject; or, in other words, they must be made so *passive*, as not to evolve a common quantity of electricity and magnetism for the brain, which state enables the operator to make up the deficiency from his superabundance; and thus feeding the brain of the subject with its life-giving elements from his own system, he gains control, for the time, over the subject's brain. The subject must be *negative*, and the operator *positive*, or the subject must be *passive*. It may be necessary that I should explain somewhat.

The action of those forces in the human body which generate Electricity, also generate Magnetism, and, as the positive power or magnetism of the subject's body must be exhausted before magnetic control can be gained over him, it is necessary that the action of these forces, or of the nerves, should be allayed, for, if not, the magnetism of the subject's body could not be exhausted.

I will now explain *why* nervous people are required for magnetic subjects. It is a fact well known to all that a person of an extreme nervous temperament is possessed of but little firmness, but is easily influenced by others; in other words, is more passive. This passiveness is induced by the weakness of the nerves, and hence enables the operator, by his will, to allay the action of the nerves, and thus infuse his own magnetism into the subject's body. Having gone thus far in explanation of the common phenomena of mesmerism, I will proceed to show you how mind *out* of the body can act upon mind *in* the body.

It was essential that I should illustrate the matter by

phenomena with which you were acquainted, in order that you might the more readily understand the explanation, which I shall now give, of the manner in which we communicate with you; for it is a fact, that all acquainted with our demonstrations must be aware of, that mesmerism and spiritual influences are closely allied in their production.

First, in explanation of the vibrations produced by us, I will say, that for *media* we must have individuals of a nervous temperament, and such as are possessed of all the requisites of a mesmeric subject. The *media* must be *passive*. The delicate organization of Spirits enables them to induce a delicate and refined species of electricity, or rather, *aromal* electricity, which, by the force of spiritual volition, they are able to throw into the system of the medium, — which immediately induces an *extra* nervous action, and hence generates *extra* quantities of *animal* electricity, which, blending with *aromal* electricity, is, by the force of our volition, thrown off from the body of the medium, to any substance that we desire, and produces the vibrations.

Aromal electricity, or electricity of our induction, is so refined, that, unless it were mingled with animal electricity, or electricity of a more gross character, it would not produce sounds; hence the necessity of a medium, and also the necessity of a medium of a peculiar temperament.

All "rapping" *media* will attest to the fact, that, while the sounds are being produced, they are in an *unnatural*, or *excited* nervous state. This is evident to any observer, from the fact of the perspiration that is frequently created in the medium, and also from the inflamed state that the hands and face often present.

It must be remembered that mesmerism is produced by a reduction or exhaustion of the magnetism of the subject's body. But, in our communications with you, —save by speaking, — we simply use the *electricity* of the body, and hence leave the medium in full possession of *all* his powers. The *positive* power is not exhausted.

Having thus briefly explained the manner in which we produce the *sounds*, I will now proceed to explain to you the phenomenon of writing. Writing *media* are of two classes, *impressible* and *mechanical*. In individuals of a peculiar temperament we are able to induce a "psychological" state of mind, and hence render their brain a channel for our thoughts and ideas. But it is seldom that we are able to find a medium so passive as to receive communications from us, in this manner, unalloyed by his own thoughts; for those who are not passive enough to be made *machines* for us to use in writing, are not sufficiently passive to receive communications from us unadulterated. *Media* of this class, and speaking *media* are the most unreliable *media* we have,—and it seldom happens that we find talking *media* who are *perfectly* reliable. A large portion of the contradictory communications received may be alleged to this class of *media* rather than to the Spirits. Our best and most reliable *media* are writing media, who are for us *machines*, and those through whom we produce the vibrations.

We do not seize the hand of the mechanical medium externally, to write, but, by the force of aromal electricity, thrown into the system of the medium, and concentrated in the arm, we for the time paralyze or destroy the nervous power of the medium's arm, and make it subservient to our will. It is well known to all that animal electricity, or nervous fluid, sent from the brain by the force of *will*, occasions a contraction of the muscular fibres, or the moving of the arm at pleasure. Now, if the forces of these electrical currents from the brain can, for a time, be suspended, or checked in any part of the *body*, the possessor has no longer power over *that portion* of the body.

This law has been taken advantage of by us in this way. Aromal electricity is thrown into the system of the medium, and concentrated in the arm in quantities sufficiently large, and in currents sufficiently rapid, as to check the power of the *animal* electricity of the brain. Hence, so long as these currents are continued by us, accompanied by *passiveness* in the medium, *we* are able to use the arm of the medium, and leave his mind as free to think as ever.

In reference to speaking *media*, I will simply say that that branch of our phenomena is produced in the same manner as mesmerism is produced by you. We take possession of the subject's natural organs, by force of electrical currents that destroy his will, and render him subservient to *our* volition.

In regard to the "tippings," I will say that they are produced on very much the same principle as is the writing. We contract the muscles of the medium's hand, and thus press upon the table, and produce, by force of large currents of animal and aromal electricity combined, the removal of objects that human strength could not, unaided, remove.

Spirits often move ponderable objects, occasion chairs to walk across the room, tables to stand suspended in mid-air, pianos to send forth their melody, untouched by human hands.

Chairs, tables, and other ponderable objects are moved by us in this manner. We immediately infiltrate the objects, we wish to move, with electricity from the body of the medium, which electricity is induced by currents passed into the body of the medium by our volition. As soon as the objects become fully charged by these currents, we are able, by other currents from the body of the medium, to impel the objects as we please, to push them upon the floor, hold them suspended in the air, &c.

There are but few *media* through whom we are able to produce demonstrations of this class, as it-requires a very *powerful nervous system*, capable of the generation of large quantities of electricity. There are fewer *media* of this class than of any other. Demonstrations of this character are intended for the satisfaction of those who measure everything by *physical*, rather than *mental* gauges.

Upon the same principle that we move ponderable objects, we play upon pianos, &c. We pass currents from the body of the medium to the different keys, as we desire, which currents move the keys, &c.

Odic lights are produced by the concentration of electrical currents from the body of the medium, which, being reduced to a *focus*, emit light.

Spirits can at times appear to you bodily; but those visits are "few and far between," as a peculiar electrical state of the medium, as well as of the atmosphere, is required.

The same conditions of atmosphere, &c., that are required for us to exhibit ourselves *bodily* to you, are required for writing unaided by the hand of a medium. For, by a concentration of electrical currents, we are able sometimes to use the pen or pencil when none are present; — but this seldom happens. Infiltrating the pen or pencil with electricity, we grasp it with our spiritual hand and write.

Thus briefly have I pointed out to you the manner in which, as well as the laws by which we communicate with you, and it may be well for me to answer a question, that short-sighted people often ask, "What is the object in these spiritual visits and communications?" In the first place allow me to state a *fact*. At this very moment two-thirds of the civilized portion of the world are atheistical, disbelieving not only the truths of the Bible, but also the existence of God,—consequently the soul's immortality. People may say this cannot be, for by far the larger portion of mankind are members of churches, or professed believers in God and religion. Does that militate against the truth of the proposition? Not at all. Does it follow, because a man is a member of a church, or a professed believer in God, &c., that he is in *reality* a believer therein? Not by any means. By what are you to determine a man's sincerity in anything? I know it has been said in Holy Writ, that "out of the abundance of the heart the mouth speaketh," but allow me to say, that if men were not *hypocrites*, this might be true; but, as the state of society is to-day, it is *not* true, for "out of the abundance of the heart the man *acteth*," and his *words* are nothing, when his words and actions do not correspond.

Now what is the fact in relation to the actions of church members and professed Christians? Your own observation will teach *you*, as mine has taught me, that not one out of a thousand of either your priests, laymen or professors, act in accordance with their teachings or professions. Now what is the inference from this? Is not the conclusion inevitable, that they are hypocrites? Most assuredly it is. Your priests go into their pulpits, and tell you that you must throw aside all worldly thoughts and pleasures, and worship God. That unless you *do* do so, you cannot merit or receive his pleasure, or salvation. Now watch that priest in his daily walks and avocations, and you will find that, in nine hundred and ninety-nine cases out of a thousand, he is *just* as avaricious, *just* as grasping, just as eager to obtain the good end of trade, just as immoral as a mere man of the world. Such too is the case with laymen and professors. They draw on a sanctimonious face for the Sabbath, go to church and *appear* mighty pious, but upon a week-day they are nothing more than men of the world,—their sanctimony is donned for the occasion.

How often do your priests have calls from *God*, to remove their fields of labor, when a little larger salary has been offered them! How often do you find a priest to have a call from *God*, that he *obeys*, when the salary offered is smaller than the one received? *Never*. The truth is, your priests preach, and your laymen listen, because of the workings of that *interest* of which I have before spoken. Mankind are hypocritical; not one of a thousand who are *professed* Christian believers, &c., are in reality *so*. Hence the idea that many *profess* to be believers in God, the immortality of the soul, &c., does not at all militate against the truth of the preceding propositions.

To relieve this atheism, and show men that there is in *reality* a God and a spiritual life for the soul, is then *one* object for which we visit you. And is there no virtue in that? Is there no benefit to be derived from a *knowledge* of the *fact* of the immortality of the soul? But we have still another object in view, and that is to show men what is their future condition, and thus enable them to live in reference thereto. Is there no benefit to be derived from that? If not, then most surely am I incapable of judging of *benefits*. We also have another object, and that is to relieve the world of the error under which it labors, and under which it has for a long period of time labored. The truth *is*, that men do not, and never have lived with reference to their spiritual life, but have sunk all other objects in physical pleasures and gratifications, and hence have detracted from the happiness which they would experience in the Spirit Land.

The religion of the world has ever taught that one could live as he or she pleased, and that if, a few moments before death, they would *repent*, they would be just as happy, just as easily saved from misery, as though they should lead moral and upright lives. Now this is a false and dangerous doctrine, and has led more than one poor soul into misery. It checks the development of the nobler attributes of the soul, and hence detracts from its happiness here; — for man, being a progressive being, is happy or unhappy here, just as he has developed and unfolded the qualities of the soul.

I will briefly sum up the objects in our communication with you, and then pass to my subject; — First, to teach men the *fact* of the soul's immortality; — Secondly, to show them the soul's future condition, and what is necessary to be done to secure happiness therefor in the Spirit Land; — Thirdly, to remove all error, and plant truth in its stead. If no benefit will accrue from all this, then perhaps our visits are useless, and need not be made. But we are inclined to believe that there is benefit to be derived from our visits in this respect; hence we shall continue to make them, until the world is changed in its moral and mental character, — until religion is based upon true principles, and society harmonized.

The various circles into which the Spirit Land is divided are not connected, but are situated one above the other, like entirely detached and separate worlds,—the First Circle being nearer the Earth than the Second, the Second nearer than the Third, &c., to the Seventh Circle or Third Sphere, which has no connection with the Earth. For the better satisfaction of the mind, I may here introduce a diagram of the Spheres and Circles. [*See opposite page.*]

The First Circle appears and *is* extremely inharmonious. The Second more harmonious than the First. The Third more harmonious than the Second, &c., until you arrive at the Seventh Circle, or Third Sphere, which is perfectly harmonious. In relation to the location of these circles, allow me to say, that all the circles, save the Seventh, are within the circle of the solar system; but the Seventh Circle, or Third Sphere, is removed beyond the circle of all systems, — in a word, it stands outside of *all worlds*, or all solar systems; hence the human mind is incapable of conceiving its locality. Each circle is situated some hundred and fifty miles from the other, making the sixth circle some 1050 miles from the Earth.

It may be asked by some, why Spirits of all worlds do not repair to the same locality? I answer, because of the difference of their states of development. The inhabitants of some worlds are so much in advance of the inhabitants of others, that even the lowest developed Spirits would not be consigned to the *highest* circles; — while the Spirits of others are not sufficiently advanced to attain even the *lowest* circles of others. The Spirits of some planets, immediately upon physical dissolution, pass to the Third Sphere, — their own planet having

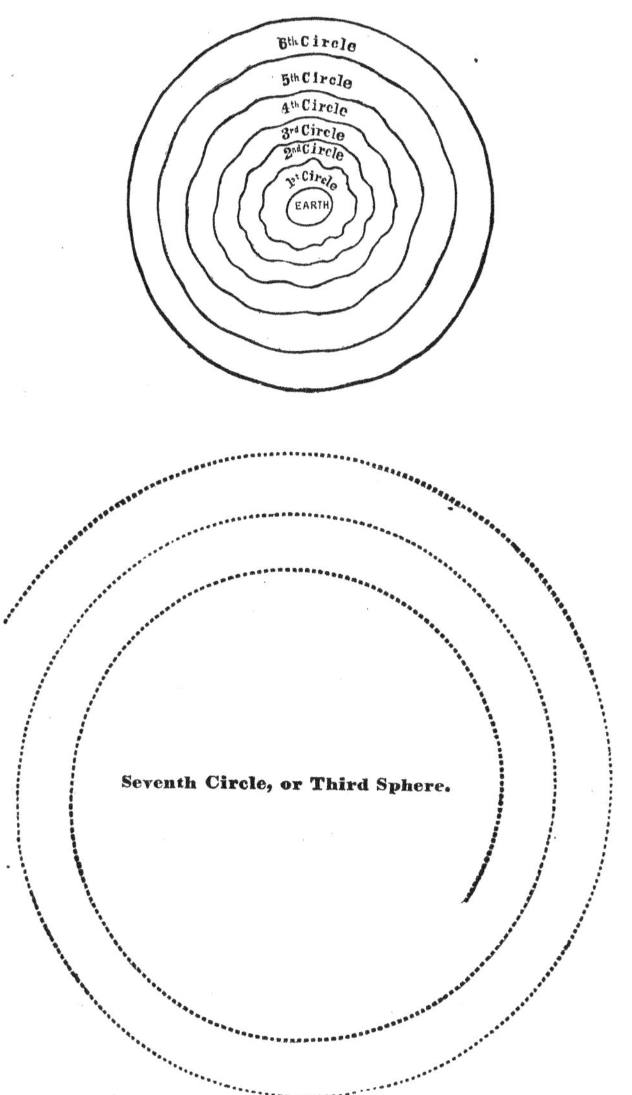
6th Circle
5th Circle
4th Circle
3rd Circle
2nd Circle
1st Circle
EARTH
Seventh Circle, or Third Sphere.

become, by the development of Spirit, the Second Sphere.

In speaking of the Spirit Land heretofore, it must be remembered, that I have spoken only of the Earth's Spirit Land; hence, when I say that the highest possible circle that the new-born Spirit can attain is the Fifth, I must be understood, — under present conditions; for that point will arrive when mankind will become so far developed, as to pass higher. But that point has not yet, nor will, for many centuries, arrive.

There are many planets whereon human life had an existence long before the Earth was evolved or developed; hence those planets are the theatres of a state of moral and mental development that the Earth is a stranger to. Of the condition of human life in many of these planets I shall speak more extensively anon.

When the inhabitants of Earth come to live more in accordance with Nature, and upon the principles of Love and Harmony, then, and not till then, will the powers of the soul become prominently developed, and the face of the universe transformed into a paradise.

It may be asked by some how Spirits regard the vicious deeds of their friends, whom, and whose deeds they can at any time have cognizance of? I answer, they regard them as frailties, and are comforted by the reflection, that that point in their lives will arrive when they will change their course of life, and progress.

THE END.

www.ingramcontent.com/pod-product-compliance
Lightning Source LLC
LaVergne TN
LVHW021422110826
845150LV00007B/2046

* 9 7 8 1 4 2 5 5 0 8 5 0 0 *